Frankenmuth's Favorite
100 Easy Chicken Breast Recipes

Best Wishes,
+ Good Cookin'
Broad from
"CHICKEN CITY USA"

That Taste Great
By: Chef John Zehnder

About The Author

John Zehnder is a third generation restaurateur, serving as Executive Chef at Zehnder's.

A 1969 graduate of the Hotel and Restaurant Management School at Michigan State University, Chef Zehnder remains active with the program. Serving on the MSU / HRI Alumni Board of Directors for many years, Zehnder was named MSU / HRI Distinguished Alumni of the Month in 1989.

Chef Zehnder is a Certified Executive Chef and winner of many culinary awards, including the prestigious "1995 Chef Professionalism Award" presented by the American Culinary Federation.

Additionally, Chef Zehnder has served as a consultant to Procter and Gamble, Noilly Prat Vermouth, The National Pork Council, The California Peach Advisory Board, the Michigan Dry Bean Council, and several other food related agencies.

Chef Zehnder oversees a kitchen staff of 125: cooks, chefs, and kitchen prep workers; plus a dining room staff of 250 servers: bartenders, hosts, and cashiers. Zehnder's is America's largest family restaurant, seating 1,500 guests and serving over one million meals each year.

Dedicated To:

My Mother
Lenore Zehnder

My first and favorite cooking teacher.

Special Thanks To:

Diane Zalewski

Table of Contents

INTRODUCTION   8

TIPS BEFORE YOU START   9

HAWAIIAN   14

GRILLED CHICKEN AND PINEAPPLE   16
RAINFOREST CHICKEN   18
COCONUT CHICKEN   20
POLYNESIAN CHICKEN KABOBS   22
MACADAMIA CRUSTED CHICKEN   24
SESAME CHICKEN   26
CAPTAIN COOK'S CHICKEN   28
CHICKEN IN SHRIMP SAUCE   30
HAWAIIAN CHICKEN VEGETABLE STIRFRY   32
MAUI CHICKEN   34

MEXICAN   36

SPANISH RICE CHICKEN   38
CHICKEN ENCHILADAS   40
CHICKEN FLAUTAS   42
ARROZ CON POLLO   44
CHICKEN TORTILLA CASSEROLE   46
WET CHICKEN BURRITOS   48
CHICKEN FAJITAS   50
CHICKEN TAMALE PIE   52
CHICKEN QUESADILLAS   54
CHICKEN TACOS   56

CAJUN   58

JAMBALAYA   60
BATON ROUGE CHICKEN   64
CHICKEN ETOUFFEE   66
MARDI GRAS CHICKEN   68

ITALIAN   70

CHICKEN PARMIGIANI   72
CHICKEN ALFREDO   74
CHICKEN TETRAZZINI   76
CHICKEN PUTENESCA   78

CHICKEN CACCIATORE	82
CHICKEN VERDE	84
CHICKEN FLORENTINE	86
CHICKEN MARSALA	88
CHICKEN PIZZAIOLA	90
FRENCH	**92**
COQ AU VIN	94
CHICKEN PARISIENNE	96
CHICKEN WITH WHITE WINE AND MUSHROOMS	98
CHICKEN AU POIVRE	100
CHICKEN MORNAY	102
CHICKEN BOIVIN	104
CHICKEN WITH MADEIRA AND ONIONS	106
CHICKEN WITH RED WINE AND SHALLOTS	108
CHICKEN WITH BRIE SAUCE	110
CHICKEN ROYAL	112
CALIFORNIAN	**114**
CHICKEN IN STRAWBERRY SAUCE	116
STIRFRY CHICKEN WITH ZUCCHINI AND SUMMER SQUASH	118
SAN DIEGO CHICKEN	120
NAPA VALLEY CHICKEN	122
CHICKEN IN MONTEREY CRAB SAUCE	124
CARIBBEAN	**126**
TRINIDAD CURRY CHICKEN	128
DOMINICAN CHICKEN IN PEPPER SAUCE	130
CALYPSO CHICKEN	132
PUERTO RICAN CHICKEN IN ORANGE SAUCE	134
HAITIAN MARINATED CHICKEN	136
CALLALO SOUP	138
JAMAICAN CHICKEN AND BANANAS	140
KINGSTON – STYLE "JERK" CHICKEN	142
CUBAN CHICKEN WITH BLACK BEANS	144
GRILLED CHICKEN WITH MANGO CHUTNEY	146
CHINESE	**148**
OYSTER SAUCED CHICKEN AND BROCCOLI	150
MU SHU CHICKEN	152
STIR-FRY CHICKEN AND MUSHROOMS	154
GINGER CHICKEN	156
CHOO CHOO TRAIN RICE	158
DRUNKEN CHICKEN	160

SOUTHERN COOKING   170

PECAN CHICKEN   172
PEACHY CHICKEN   174
SOUTHERN FRIED CHICKEN   176
CHICKEN FRIED CHICKEN   178
CORN MEAL CHICKEN   180

FLORIDA – STYLE   182

CHICKEN WITH ORANGE SEGMENTS   184
FLORIDA GRAPEFRUIT CHICKEN   186
FLORIDA LEMON ZEST CHICKEN   188
AVOCADO CHICKEN SAUTÉ   190
ORANGE BASTED CHICKEN   192

TEX-MEX   194

BARBECUED CHICKEN   196
JALAPENOS CHICKEN   198
EL PASO CHICKEN   200
SAN ANTONIO CHICKEN   202
HOT SALSA CHICKEN   204

MIDWEST "HEARTLAND"   206

CHICKEN AND APPLES   208
MICHIGAN CHERRY SAUCED CHICKEN   210
EASY WISCONSIN CHICKEN   212
CHICAGO STYLE CHICKEN   214
MILWAUKEE STYLE CHICKEN   216

AMISH COUNTRY   218

HOT CHICKEN SALAD   220
LANCASTER CHICKEN SALAD   222
CHICKEN AND APPLE SALAD   224
CHICKEN IN SOUR CREAM SAUCE   226
POACHED CHICKEN AND VEGETABLES   228

AMERICAN "QUICK DISH"   **230**

CORN FLAKE CHICKEN   232
CHICKEN AND NOODLE BAKE   234
CRUNCHY ONION CHICKEN   236
MARINATED BROILED CHICKEN   238
LEMON CHICKEN   240

METRIC CONVERSIONS   **241**

Introduction

Frankenmuth – chicken the terms are interchangeable in many people's mind. In this cookbook the focus is on that noble of all birds!

Chicken Breast is to a chef what canvas is to a painter. It is the medium in which the only limitations are in the mind of a cook or chef.

"What are you hungry for?" How many times have you heard that phrase. I have the recipes listed by country or region, allowing you to pick and choose based on your cravings. You can prepare recipes with chicken everyday for two weeks and have different tastes each night.

The spices listed in the recipes are true to the cuisine on the country or region represented. Many home cooks simply don't add the spices if they don't have them in their cupboards. You'll be doing yourself a disservice if you omit spices! Cooking with just salt and pepper is like an artist who only paints in black and white. Spices add color and character to food.

Finally, thoughts of "Diet Food" are normally associated with chicken breasts. I make no claims of low calorie – low fat. My chicken recipes are good tasting dishes containing some oil and butter. Most take minimal time to prepare and in this hectic world that's a real plus!

You are about to take a culinary tour of the world. I hope you enjoy the trip!!

Tips Before You Start

<u>Chicken Breast</u> My recipes all call for boneless, skinless chicken breast. I would suggest that you pound each breast so that it is the same thickness in the center as on the edges. Insuring that each piece cooks uniformly. When working with chicken it is imperative that you rinse each piece with cool water and don't expose other food or kitchen surfaces to the raw chicken. Salmonella, a food born illness, is common on chicken and can be passed to other foods. Since salmonella is killed at 170° proper cooking will eliminate any risks.

<u>Thickening Agents</u> We'll be working with natural food products that contain differing amounts of water. Additionally, cornstarch and flour contain varying amounts of starch. The difference between brands is not normally dramatic, but it can be. When using thickening agents you need to go by look – adding or decreasing amounts of thickeners until you get the right consistency. Cornstarch will "Thin Out" if you hold it at a high temperature for more than ten minutes. In this case a little extra cornstarch will return the product to the correct thickness. Always use cold water when mixing thickeners.

Cooking Oil/butter Many of the recipes list both butter and oil for sautéing. The reason we use a combination is that butter, used alone, will burn because of its low smoke point. Vegetable oil added to butter allows you to sauté at a higher temperature without burning. Unless specified, the vegetable oil that I recommend is Canola Oil. Soybean or sunflower oil also work, but may import additional flavors to you recipes.

Pots and Pans The large skillet referred to in many recipes is a 10 ½ inch skillet with two inch sides. Saucepans vary in size, but I recommend a 3 quart. Casserole dishes in the recipes are the four-inch deep ceramic dishes that hold 3 quarts.

Salt The amounts listed in each recipe will vary. Recipes with olives, capers, and ham will add salt naturally, so they have little to no salt added. Salt tolerance varies from person to person. I have purposely kept the salt amounts to a minimum. Add more if you like.

Spices Ideally fresh spices should be used, but I realize that it is not always possible for the spices listed in each recipe therefore, refer to the dry varieties common in all grocery stores.

<u>Pepper</u> Moderate amounts of pepper are in the recipes. If you are sensitive to pepper, use a little less. Black pepper is robust, white pepper is a bit milder and is often used when you don't want to see specks in your dish, especially white sauces. Cayenne pepper is the hot one. It gives Mexican and Tex-Mex foods their bite.

<u>Chicken Broth</u> Using chicken broth will always give the best results. However, chicken bouillon can be substituted. Bouillon will give your recipes a saltier taste.

<u>Rice</u> You can use converted rice in any of the recipes. Long grain rice will take slightly longer to cook but, I feel it stands up to prolonged cooking temperatures better. The recipes will specify when to use long grain. Do not use the instant rice varieties in these recipes. Instant rice will give you a mushy product.

Deglazing a Pan Some of the recipes refer to pouring liquid into a skillet in which chicken breasts have been sautéed. Stirring up the browned particles on the surface of the skillet is important in that these particles add flavors. In culinary terms we call this process "deglazing."

Remember! A recipe is a road map, sometimes you have to detour, other times it is fun to take a side road to see where it may lead. Experiment with the recipes and customize them to your personal tastes. Don't feel obligated to a written recipe. After all, you have to eat it!

Hawaiian

The First stop on our culinary tour is Hawaii. The lure of secluded

lagoons, swaying palm trees, and black sand beaches is almost irresistible.

A melting pot of many ethnic groups, Hawaii has embraced the
cultures to create its own unique foods.

Pineapples, bananas, coconuts, and macadamia nuts are used in this

series of recipes. I like the fact that Hawaiian recipes use fruit in every

course. The fresh, tart flavors of tropical fruits are perfect with chicken. I

hope you agree.

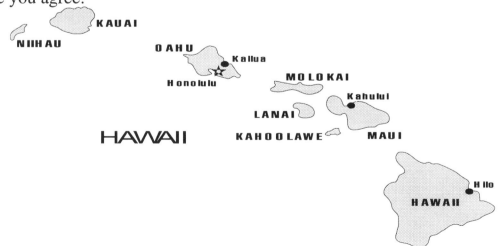

Grapeseed oil comes from pressed grapeseeds discarded in the wine making process. Common in the Mediterranean, grapeseed oil has gained attention because it has a smoke point at 420. This means that it can withstand the high heat associated with quick sautés and stir fries. Somewhat neutral in flavor, grapeseed oil will add little noticeable flavor to you recipes.

Recipe Notes

_____

_____

_____

_____

_____

_____

_____

_____

_____

_____

_____

_____

_____

_____

_____

Grilled Chicken and Pineapple

4 (6oz.)	chicken breast
2 TBSP.	vegetable oil
1 TBSP.	butter
1	fresh whole pineapple
½ c.	brown sugar
1 TBSP.	butter

Method:

♦ Cut top off ripe pineapple and trim off rough outside skin of the

   pineapple. Split pineapple in half – lengthwise.

♦ Heat oil and butter to medium heat. Place chicken in skillet and sauté 3 –

   4 minutes on each side until done.

♦ Cut pineapple into half-inch slices.

♦ Wipe out skillet in which you sautéed chicken.

♦ Heat butter into skillet at medium heat. Spread across entire surface of

   skillet.

♦ Place pineapple slices in skillet. Sprinkle each slice with brown sugar.

♦ Set chicken breast on pineapple slices.

♦ Grill for 1 ½ - 2 minutes.

♦ Remove from skillet with large spatula, flipping each chicken piece over

   as you remove from pan so pineapple slices are on top.

♦ Serve.

One of the most frequently asked questions about food preparation is, "What is the difference between a herb and a spice?" After thirty years of searching, I've come to the conclusion the terms are used interchangeably. Leaves, seeds, twigs, roots and bark are all called herbs or spices. Along with recipes, I'd like to present you with some history and tradition associated with spices and herbs. I hope you will find this information as interesting as I do.

Recipe Notes

_____

_____

_____

_____

_____

_____

_____

_____

_____

_____

_____

_____

_____

_____

_____

_____

_____

Rainforest Chicken

4 (6oz.)	chicken breasts
1 TBSP.	vegetable oil
1 TBSP.	butter
¼ lb.	butter
½ c.	sugar
½ c.	brown sugar
¼ c.	light rum
2	yellow bananas – not quite ripe

Method:

♦ Sauté chicken breasts in oil and butter, in large skillet, 3 – 4 minutes.

♦ Remove chicken from skillet and set aside.

♦ Wipe out skillet and add remaining butter and melt.

♦ At medium heat stir in sugar and brown sugar. Continue to heat.

♦ 4– 5 minutes, stirring constantly.

♦ Pour in rum and add bananas that have been cut into ½-inch slices.

♦ Simmer for 2 – 3 minutes while stirring.

♦ Place chicken in banana sauce and coat each piece of chicken.

♦ Simmer until chicken is hot (1-2 minutes).

♦ Serve.

Most of the spices we use today began as the medicines of ancient civilizations. All cultures, worldwide, use spices and herbs. Many cultures still use spices and herbs as medicine. Modern drugs can trace there roots to jungle herbs. Pharmaceutical companies still employ pharmacists and doctors whose job it is to research herb remedies and native potions.

Recipe Notes

_____
_____
_____
_____
_____
_____
_____
_____
_____
_____
_____
_____
_____
_____
_____
_____

Coconut Chicken

3	eggs
½ c.	milk
½ c.	coconut milk
1 c.	coconut unsweetened shredded
½ c.	all purpose flour
4 (6oz.)	chicken breasts
2 TBSP.	vegetable oil
1 TBSP.	butter

Method:

♦ Mix eggs, milk, and coconut milk in a large bowl.

♦ Pound chicken to ½-inch thickness, between two pieces of wax paper, using the flat side of a knife blade.

♦ Dip chicken into egg and milk mixture.

♦ Combine coconut and flour. Dredge chicken in coconut.

♦ Allow to dry for five minutes.

♦ Heat oil and butter in large skillet to medium heat.

♦ Sauté chicken in skillet 2 - 3 minutes on each side until golden brown.

♦ Serve.

Kitchen cupboards in ancient Greece and Rome had many of the same spices/herbs found in the modern American grocery store. Mustard, oregano, bay leaves, basil were all commonly used 3000 years ago. When it comes to cooking nothing much has changed in the spice/herb category.

Recipe Notes

_____
_____
_____
_____
_____
_____
_____
_____
_____
_____
_____
_____
_____
_____
_____
_____
_____

Polynesian Chicken Kabobs

4 (6oz.)	chicken breasts
3 c.	pineapple juice
½ tsp.	ginger
1 can	pineapple chunks
1	cantaloupe
1	honeydew melon
12	6-inch wood skewers

Method:

♦ Pour pineapple juice in large skillet. Add ginger, bring to boil.

♦ Place chicken breasts in pineapple juice and simmer 10 – 12 minutes – until done.

♦ Chill chicken breasts for one hour.

♦ Using a melon baller, cut melons into balls.

♦ Cut chilled chicken into one-inch squares.

♦ Arrange as follows: chicken, cantaloupe, chicken, honeydew, chicken, pineapple chunks.

♦ Serve as luncheon item or appetizer.

Spice caravans with as many as 4000 camels crossed the deserts 2000 years before Christ, bringing with them treasures more precious than gold. Rare and exotic spices were used by the rich and powerful to season their foods and heal their ills. Crusaders in the middle ages searched as much to find the spice routes as they did to save the holy lands from Muslim invaders. A pound of cloves could have bought you a half dozen horses in Caesar's Rome.

Recipe Notes

_____
_____
_____
_____
_____
_____
_____
_____
_____
_____
_____
_____
_____
_____
_____

Macadamia Crusted Chicken

4 (6oz.)	chicken breast
2 TBSP.	vegetable oil
1 TBSP.	butter
¾ c.	crushed macadamia nuts
2 c.	crushed corn flakes
3	eggs
1 c.	milk

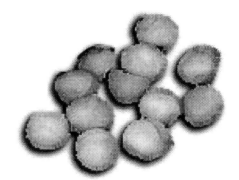

Method:

♦ Pound chicken to ½ inch thick between two pieces of wax paper.

♦ Whisk eggs and milk together in large bowl.

♦ Dip chicken in egg and milk mixture. Allow excess to drip off.

♦ Lay chicken in mixture of nuts and corn flakes, coating both sides evenly.

♦ Refrigerate for ½ hour separating chicken with wax paper.

♦ Heat oil and butter in large skillet to medium heat.

♦ Sauté chicken 2 – 3 minutes on each side until golden brown.

♦ Serve.

Roman soldiers, in ancient times, were often paid in spices and salt rather than money. Soldiers easily could exchange their prized booty for anything they needed especially in foreign countries where luxuries were non-existent even among the wealthy. A favorite beverage of the roman army was mead. A wine made with honey and spices.

Recipe Notes

_____

_____

_____

_____

_____

_____

_____

_____

_____

_____

_____

_____

_____

_____

_____

Sesame Chicken

4 (6oz.)	chicken breast
1 c.	honey
1/3 c.	lime juice
1/3 c.	orange juice
1 TBSP.	butter
1 ½ TBSP.	sesame seeds

Method:

♦ Place chicken breast on broiler tray and broil at low heat 2 – 3 minutes on each side.

♦ Put honey, lime juice, orange juice, and butter in a small saucepan. Heat to boiling.

♦ Remove from heat and add sesame seeds.

♦ Baste half done chicken with sauce, spreading sesame seeds evenly across chicken.

♦ Return to low broiler heat for 4 – 5 minutes on each side, basting frequently.

♦ Remove from broiler and serve.

"One man's meat is anothers' poison." Cultures develop their own preference for herbs/spices. History and tradition often dictate which spices are favored. On the other hand, many spices are cross-cultural. Bay leaves, cumin, pepper, and oregano are used throughout the world creating a wide array of dishes and tastes. An old Chinese blessing says, "May you always be healthy and have a full spice jar."

Recipe Notes

_____

_____

_____

_____

_____

_____

_____

_____

_____

_____

_____

_____

_____

_____

_____

Captain Cook's Chicken

½ c.	water chestnuts	2 TBSP.	brown sugar
¾ c.	Chinese cabbage – ½ " cut	2 TBSP.	white vinegar
½ c.	carrots – ¼ " cut	1 TBSP.	soy sauce
½ c.	bamboo shoots	2 c.	chicken broth
2 ½ c.	chicken breast-½" cuts cooked	3 TBSP.	corn starch
2 TBSP.	vegetable oil	4 TBSP.	cold water

Method:

♦ Heat oil in large skillet to medium heat.

♦ Add water chestnuts, cabbage, carrots, and bamboo shoots. Sauté for 4 –

5 minutes.

♦ Add chicken pieces and stir in.

♦ Mix in brown sugar, vinegar, soy, and chicken broth.

♦ Bring to boil.

♦ Mix cornstarch and cold water until smooth.

♦ Slowly pour into boiling chicken and vegetables.

♦ Stir while returning to boil and mix thickens.

♦ Serve over rice or chow mein noodles.

You get what you pay for! When it comes to spices no truer words have ever been spoken. Prices vary depending on where the spice was grown and how carefully it was handled, spices have different potency. If you have to use twice as much cheaper spice as the expensive to get the same great taste is it really a bargain?

Recipe Notes

_____

_____

_____

_____

_____

_____

_____

_____

_____

_____

_____

_____

_____

_____

Chicken in Shrimp Sauce

4 (6oz.)	chicken breast
1 TBSP.	butter
1 TBSP.	vegetable oil
1 ½ c.	milk
1 ½ c.	chicken broth
2 tsp.	paprika
2 tsp.	salt
½ tsp.	ground black pepper
1 c.	small salad-type shrimp
3 TBSP.	flour
3 TBSP.	cold water

Method:

♦ Sauté chicken in large skillet 2 – 3 minutes on each side. Remove from skillet.

♦ Pour milk, broth in same skillet. Add salt and spices. Bring to boil.

♦ Mix flour and water. Slowly whisk into boiling milk – broth until thickened.

♦ Add shrimp and stir in.

♦ Place chicken in deep casserole dish. Pour sauce over chicken.

♦ Cover and bake for 25 minutes at 325°.

When you purchase dry spices look for good color and a minimum of "dusty" residue on the bottom of the container. When opened the spice should have a sharp aroma. After using, close container tight. The best way to insure consistent flavor is to use a good spice, the same brand, all the time.

Recipe Notes

Hawaiian Chicken Vegetable StirFry

4 (6oz.)	chicken breasts
1 TBSP.	vegetable oil
1 TBSP.	soy sauce
1 c.	pineapple chunks
1 c.	snow peas
½ c.	water chestnuts
1 TBSP.	cornstarch
1 TBSP.	cold water

Method:

♦ Cut raw chicken into ½" strips.

♦ Heat wok to high heat. Stir-fry chicken for 2 – 3 minutes. Remove from wok, set aside.

♦ Wipe out wok and preheat to hot.

♦ Add one-tablespoon oil. Add pineapple, snow peas, soy sauce and chestnuts. Stir-fry 2 – 3 minutes – snowpeas will soften but be crisp.

♦ Stir in cornstarch and cold water in vegetables. Coat vegetables.

♦ Return chicken to wok and toss 1 – 2 minutes, mixing all ingredients together.

♦ Serve with rice or chow mein noodles.

Spices, unlike good wine, do not improve with age. The older the spice the less flavor it will have. Even the best spices will decrease in aroma quality over a period of time. That pumpkin pie spice you bought three years ago isn't the same any more, throw it out! Spices are inexpensive compared to all your other recipe ingredients. Why compromise your cooking?

Recipe Notes

_____

_____

_____

_____

_____

_____

_____

_____

_____

_____

_____

_____

_____

_____

_____

_____

Maui Chicken

4 (6oz.)	chicken breast
2	yellow bananas - not quite ripe
4	3 oz. lean ham slices
1 c.	flour
1 c.	coconut
3	eggs
1 c.	milk

Method:

♦ Place chicken breast between sheets of waxed paper and pound to ¼ inch thick.

♦ Cut each banana lengthwise into quarters.

♦ Wrap ham slices around bananas.

♦ Place ham wrapped bananas in center of pounded chicken breast.

♦ Roll chicken breast around ham / banana. Pick with toothpick to hold in place.

♦ Roll in flour and then dip into egg/milk mix.

♦ Roll in coconut.

♦ Refrigerate one hour.

♦ Deep fry 3 – 4 minutes at 350°

♦ Serve with sweet and sour sauce.

Mexican

Mexican Cuisine, just a few years ago this style of cooking seemed strange and exotic. Now days, Mexican restaurants or fast food places are everywhere you look!

MEXICO

The basic ingredients in most Mexican cooking are tomatoes, cumin, cilantro, cayenne pepper and the ever-present tortilla. I've used corn oil in most of my recipes, it adds an authentic taste to the dishes

Chilis are a new world discovery which quickly spreads across the globe, called peppers by Columbus and his crew. Chilis actually belong to a family of plants named capsicums. Ranked by "heat" the general rule is- the smaller the chili, the bigger the bite.

Recipe Notes

_____

_____

_____

_____

_____

_____

_____

_____

_____

_____

_____

_____

_____

_____

_____

♦ Spanish Rice Chicken

2 c.	long grain rice
2 c.	tomato juice
2 c.	chicken broth
1 tsp.	salt
2 tsp.	cumin
½ tsp.	cayenne pepper
1 tsp.	cilantro
1 tsp.	chopped garlic
½ c.	corn oil
4 (6oz.)	chicken breast

Method:

♦ Mix juice, broth, salt, spices, and garlic in saucepan.

♦ Place rice in deep baking dish.

♦ Heat until boiling – Remove from heat.

♦ Add corn oil to skillet and brown chicken breast on both sides. Remove breast from skillet.

♦ Pour hot tomato sauce over rice and stir until blended. Make certain there is 2-inch space between rice and top of baking dish.

♦ Place browned chicken on top of sauce – rice. Breast will be floating in liquid.

♦ Cover baking dish and bake 50 minutes at 350°. Dish is done when rice is soft.

All chilis begin as green pods and ripen into reds, yellows, and browns. Green chilis are roasted and then cut into pieces to use in recipes. Ripe chilis are dried and crushed/broken into the food. Dried bunches of chilis are called ristras and remain potent for many months. Hanging ristras are a common sight throughout the southwest.

Recipe Notes

_____

_____

_____

_____

_____

_____

_____

_____

_____

_____

_____

_____

_____

_____

_____

_____

Chicken Enchiladas

Enchilada Sauce

3 TBSP.	corn oil	4 TBSP.	chili powder
3 TBSP.	all purpose flour	¼ tsp.	garlic salt
2 c	water	1 tsp.	salt

Method:

♦ Heat oil to medium in skillet

♦ Add flour and brown to caramel color stirring constantly.

♦ Add water, spices and salt to oil / flour.

♦ Whisk with wire whip and heat to boiling.

♦ The sauces should have a gravy consistency.

3 TBSP.	corn oil	4 (6 oz.)	chicken breast cooked
6	corn tortillas		cut in ½" strips.
1 c.	shredded taco cheese		

Method:

♦ Heat oil in large skillet to medium heat.

♦ Lay tortillas flat on countertop.

♦ Lay chicken strips lengthwise in center of tortillas.

♦ Sprinkle each chicken tortilla with cheese.

♦ Roll ends of tortilla around chicken.

♦ Place tortillas in skillet. Rolled end down in oil.

♦ Lightly brown on both sides then remove from skillet.

♦ Drain on paper towel and place - single file – in shallow baking dish.

♦ Pour over sauce and bake 15 minutes in 350° oven.

♦ Remove from oven and top with shredded lettuce and diced tomatoes.

The long pointed poblano verda chili is first choice for classic chilis rellenos. Mild flavored and low in heat. These chilis are also used in salsa and soups. The dried version of this chili is called ancho.

Recipe Notes

_____

_____

_____

_____

_____

_____

_____

_____

_____

_____

_____

_____

_____

_____

Chicken Flautas

4 TBSP.	butter		1 tsp.	cumin
1 TBSP.	corn oil		1 TBSP.	lemon juice
¼ c.	flour		½ c.	black olives - sliced
2 TBSP.	fine diced onion		½ c.	corn oil
¼ tsp.	paprika		12	flour tortillas
1 tsp.	salt			
1 c.	cooked chicken breast – diced			

Method:

♦ Heat butter in saucepan, add onions and sauté until soft, add flour and stir. Pour corn oil into butter / onion mixture.

♦ Stir in paprika, salt, cumin, lemon juice and black olives. Heat 2 – 3 minutes.

♦ Add diced chicken – if stiff soften with warm water – should have soft not runny consistency.

♦ Set aside in refrigerator for a half-hour.

♦ Heat corn oil to medium heat in skillet.

♦ Place one tablespoon chicken mixture lengthwise in center of flour tortilla.

♦ Roll tortilla around chicken mixture tightly and pick with wooden toothpick.

♦ Fry in corn oil until browned, yet still soft.

♦ Drain on paper towel.

♦ Dip in your favorite salsa or guacamole.

The anaheim red chili is a long flat chili with mild heat. Salsa and chilis rellenos are its primary use. Another milder chili is the DeAgua, a medium sized pointed pepper used in moles and soups.

Recipe Notes

_____

_____

_____

_____

_____

_____

_____

_____

_____

_____

_____

_____

_____

_____

_____

Arroz con Pollo

3 TBSP.	corn oil		½ tsp.	black pepper (ground)
2 ½ c.	long grain rice		½ tsp.	salt
2 TBSP.	onion – Spanish – diced		½ tsp.	garlic salt
3 TBSP.	green pepper – diced		6 oz.	tomato sauce
5 c.	chicken broth		2 c.	diced cooked chicken

Method:

♦ Heat oil in skillet to medium heat, add rice and brown – stirring constantly.

♦ Add onions and green pepper – continue to sauté 2 – 3 minutes.

♦ Pour in broth, spices and tomato sauce.

♦ Stir until blended.

♦ Simmer for 50 – 60 minutes – covered.

♦ When rice is soft, add chicken – stir in.

♦ Remove from heat – leave covered for 5 minutes.

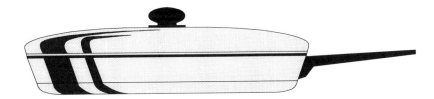

The Jalapena and Guero chilis are slightly smaller than the DeAgua. Surprisingly, these chilis are about in the middle range when it comes to heat. The Guero is a round yellow chili used for moles and sauces. Jalapenas are usually sold pickled, north of Texas.

Recipe Notes

_____

_____

_____

_____

_____

_____

_____

_____

_____

_____

_____

_____

_____

_____

_____

_____

Chicken Tortilla Casserole

2 c.	cooked elbow macaroni	1 tsp.	cayenne pepper
1 c.	evaporated milk	1 ½ c.	shredded taco cheese
1 tsp.	cilantro		
1 tsp.	oregano	3 c.	crushed corn taco shells
2 TBSP.	butter		
½ tsp.	garlic salt	2 c.	diced chicken breast cooked
2 tsp.	salt		
2 c.	tomato sauce	1 c.	mild salsa

Method:

♦ Mix all ingredients together except for cheese and butter.

♦ Once mixed, stir in cheese – blend evenly.

♦ Butter 1-½ quart casserole dish – bottom and sides.

♦ Pour in casserole mixture.

♦ Bake at 350° for 20 minutes or until cheese bubbles.

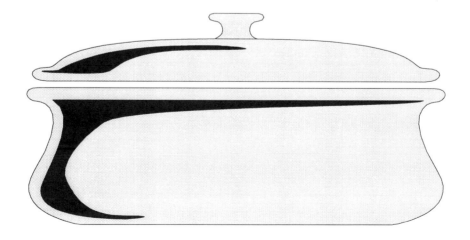

Red Serrano is a small tubular shaped chili native to Mexico. Pickled or used in salsas. We're starting to get some "heat". The red serrano is classified as a medium hot chili. Small pea-like tepin chilis are in the same range as the serrano and are used carefully in salsa.

Recipe Notes

Wet Chicken Burritos

4 (6 oz.)	raw chicken breast - ½" strips	½ tsp.	cumin
¼ c.	corn oil	1 tsp.	salt
8 lg.	Flour tortillas		

Method:

♦ Heat oil in skillet to medium heat.

♦ Add chicken strips and seasonings.

♦ Sauté until chicken is done (5 – 8 minutes).

Burrito Sauce

2 tsp.	corn oil	½ tsp.	garlic salt
5	ripe tomatoes – diced	½ tsp.	oregano
3	green chilis – chopped	6 oz.	tomato sauce
½ c.	shredded taco cheese		

Method:

♦ Heat oil in skillet to medium heat.

♦ Sauté tomatoes and chilis until soft and tender.

♦ Add seasonings, cheese and simmer 5 minutes.

♦ Sauce should be smooth and medium thick.

Preparation

♦ Lay 8 large flour tortillas flat on countertop.

♦ Fill center of tortillas with chicken mixture.

♦ Fold edges to center forming a pillow shape.

♦ Lay folded edges face down in baking dish.

♦ Pour over sauce

♦ Bake at 350° for 8 – 10 minutes, cheese will bubble.

♦ Remove from oven and serve.

In addition to heat, chipotle chilis have an unusual flavor. Its small shape is similar to a jalapena chili. Chipotle chilis have a smoky flavor that distinctively flavors any dish to which it is added.

Recipe Notes

_____

_____

_____

_____

_____

_____

_____

_____

_____

_____

_____

_____

_____

_____

_____

_____

_____

Chicken Fajitas

2	green peppers – cut in ½" strips	2 tsp.	cumin
1	red pepper - cut in ½" strips	1 tsp.	cilantro
1	Spanish onion - cut in ½" strips	1 tsp.	cayenne pepper
4 (6 oz.)	chicken breast - cut in ½" strips	1 tsp.	oregano
½ c.	corn oil	2 tsp.	salt
6 lg.	flour tortillas		

Method:

♦ Heat oil to medium heat in large skillet.

♦ Add chicken breast strips and sauté on high heat until 3 quarters done.

♦ Add peppers and onion to skillet.

♦ Mix all spices and salt together.

♦ Sprinkle seasonings on chicken – peppers – onions.

♦ Sauté until peppers and onions are soft.

♦ Heat skillet to medium heat – heat tortillas on both sides – no oil.

♦ Remove tortillas from skillet and fill center lengthwise with chicken – onions – peppers.

♦ Top with salsa, guacamole, and sour cream.

Next to pepper, the most commonly used spice is cumin. Cultures world wide have embraced the aromatic flavor of cumin. A main ingredient in chili powder. Most Americans think of cumin as "that Mexican taste".

Recipe Notes

_____

_____

_____

_____

_____

_____

_____

_____

_____

_____

_____

_____

_____

_____

_____

Chicken Tamale Pie

| 1 ¼ c. | instant corn meal | 2 TBSP. | corn oil |
| 2/3 c. | water | 2 tsp. | chili powder |

Method for crust:

♦ Combine all ingredients in mixing bowl until well blended.

♦ Butter bottom and sides of 1 ½ quart casserole dish.

♦ Spread crust mixture evenly on bottom and sides of casserole dish.

2 ½ c.	diced cooked chicken	15 oz. can	creamed corn
1 c.	onion – diced	4 oz.	chilis - chopped
1 tsp.	garlic – chopped	½ c.	black olives sliced
1 tsp.	salt	1 c.	shredded mild
¼ tsp.	cayenne pepper		cheese

Method:

♦ In a large skillet place chicken, onions and spices.

♦ Sauté 3 – 4 minutes – add a small amount of corn oil if mixture is sticking.

♦ Add corn, chilis and olives – mix all ingredients well. Heat until mixture is hot.

♦ Pour into crust lined pan.

♦ Bake at 375° for 20 minutes.

♦ Sprinkle cheese on top of casserole.

♦ Return to oven until cheese melts and bubbles.

♦ Remove from oven, let set for 5 minutes before cutting.

Cumin, according to fable and folklore, prevented a husband from wandering. Keeping a few cumin seeds in you apron, it said, will insure your spouse is faithful. Cumin seeds mixed with feed was also suppose to stop chickens from straying out of the yard. Who knows, maybe it works!

Recipe Notes

_____

_____

_____

_____

_____

_____

_____

_____

_____

_____

_____

_____

_____

_____

Chicken Quesadillas

¼ c.	corn oil	12	flour tortillas
4 (6 oz.)	chicken breast - cut in ½" strips	1 c.	shredded taco cheese
1 tsp.	cumin	1 c.	diced fresh tomatoes
1 tsp.	salt	2	japelenas cut 1/8" thick
1 tsp.	cilantro		
½ c.	corn oil		

Method:

♦ Heat ¼ c. corn oil in a skillet.

♦ Add chicken breast strips and season with spices and salt.

♦ Sauté 5 – 8 minutes at medium heat – until chicken is done.

♦ Lay six tortillas flat on countertop.

♦ Divide chicken strips by six and spread across surface of the 6 tortillas.

♦ Scatter shredded cheese on chicken strips.

♦ Divide tomatoes across top of chicken and cheese.

♦ Place japalenas on top of tomatoes – be careful they're hot. Top with second tortilla shell.

♦ Add enough corn oil to skillet to coat surface of pan.

♦ Grill tortillas until light brown on both sides. Cheese will melt. Cut into quarters.

♦ Serve with green chili salsa, guacamole and sour cream.

Chili powder-not a single spice but a blend of garlic, cumin. oregano, and chilis. Chili powders were used by the Aztecs in Mexico and central America centuries before European explorers first set foot on western soil. Chili powders can be used in specialty dishes or simply as seasoning on hamburgers, eggs, gravies, and sauces.

Recipe Notes

Chicken Tacos

4 (6 oz.)	chicken breast - cut in ½" strips	8	soft flour tortillas
1 ½ tsp.	cumin	1 c.	shredded taco cheese
1 tsp.	cilantro		
1 tsp.	oregano	2 c.	shredded lettuce
2 tsp.	garlic – chopped	1 c.	diced rip tomatoes
1 ½ tsp.	salt		sour cream
1 tsp.	cayenne pepper		salsa
½ c.	corn oil		guacamole

Method:

♦ Pour corn oil into large skillet and heat to medium heat.

♦ Add chicken strips to oil – begin to sauté.

♦ Mix all spices and salt together.

♦ Sprinkle this seasoning mix over chicken breast strips.

♦ Sauté chicken with spices until chicken is done (5 – 8 minutes). Add

small amount of water if dry.

♦ Put an equal amount of chicken in the center of each tortilla and top with

cheese.

♦ Place in oven at 350° for 5 – 6 minutes – until cheese melts.

♦ Remove from oven – top with lettuce and tomatoes.

♦ Fix as you like them – with salsa, sour cream or guacamole.

Cajun

Cajun cooking is often misunderstood! Spicy and flavorful, most Cajun dishes are not overly hot. Add Tabasco if you desire more heat.

Cajun cooking usually includes "The Trinity", as chef Paul Prudhomme calls it. These three elements are peppers, onions, garlic, Bay leaves, grown in the Bayous, are also commonly added.

From a culinary perspective, New Orleans is my favorite place to visit. With so many great foods it is hard to choose which ones to eat!

Maybe that's why I keep going back!

File- secret gumbo ingredient! Bayou Indians taught Cajun settlers how to grind sassafras leaves to a powder for use in soups and stews. Added at the absolute last minute, file thickens and flavors a gumbo. Added too early and file forms unsightly strings of goo on the surface of boiling gumbo, ruining dinner.

Recipe Notes

_____

_____

_____

_____

_____

_____

_____

_____

_____

_____

_____

_____

_____

_____

Jambalaya

3 (6 oz.)	chicken breast – ½" diced raw
4 TBSP.	butter
1 c.	tomato sauce
2 c.	chopped green onions
1 c.	chopped green peppers
1 TBSP.	crushed garlic
½ tsp.	thyme
1	bay leaf crushed
2 c.	chicken broth
1 c.	long grain rice
2 tsp.	salt
1 tsp.	cayenne pepper

Method:

♦ Place butter and tomato sauce in large saucepan.

♦ Heat slowly to medium heat and continue simmering ten minutes.

♦ Add the chicken, peppers, onions and garlic. Stir constantly and heat for ten minutes.

♦ Pour in the broth and spices. Heat to boiling.

♦ Add rice and stir – heat five minutes, covered.

♦ Pour all mixture in a Dutch oven type casserole dish with cover.

♦ Cover dish and bake at 350° for 45 minutes.

♦ Uncover and stir jambalaya before serving.

Bay leaves grow throughout the world. Romans awarded heros and athletes with crowns made from bay leaves. Cajuns discovered bay leaves growing wild in the bayous of Louisiana and quickly incorporated them into many of their recipes.

Recipe Notes

_____

_____

_____

_____

_____

_____

_____

_____

_____

_____

_____

_____

_____

_____

_____

_____

Baton Rouge Chicken

4 (6 oz.)	chicken breast – ¼" strips raw
2 TBSP.	butter
1 TBSP.	vegetable oil
2	green peppers – ½" strips
1	red pepper – ½" strips
12	green onions – ½" cuts
1 tsp.	thyme
½ tsp.	crushed bay leaf
½ tsp.	cayenne pepper
1 ½ tsp.	salt

Method:

♦ Place butter and oil in large skillet. Heat to medium heat – do not burn

oil.

♦ Add chicken strips and stir-fry for 3 – 4 minutes.

♦ Add peppers and green onions. Turn heat to high and stir-fry for 2 – 3

minutes.

♦ Half way through the cooking time add spices and salt

♦ Serve with rice or pasta.

Bees pollinating the thyme near Athens produced a honey considered a delicacy to ancient Greece. Medieval knights carried bouquets of thyme into battle to give them courage and valor. Today this fragrant and aromatic herb is used to season soups. Clam chowders and oyster stew are never quite right without a touch of thyme.

Recipe Notes

_____

_____

_____

_____

_____

_____

_____

_____

_____

_____

_____

_____

_____

_____

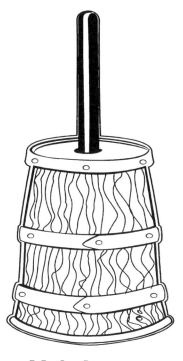

Chicken Creole

2 TBSP.	butter
4 (6 oz.)	chicken breast – ½" strips
12	green onions – ½" strips
1	red pepper – ½" strips
1	green peppers – ½" strips
1 TBSP.	crushed garlic
12 oz	tomato sauce
1	bay leaves whole
2 tsp.	oregano
1 tsp.	thyme
½ - 1 c.	chicken broth – as needed
1 TBSP.	cornstarch
2 TBSP.	water

Method:

♦ Place butter in large skillet. Heat until butter melts and is bubbly.

♦ Add chicken breast and sauté 2 – 3 minutes. Add onions, peppers and garlic. Continue to sauté until peppers are limp.

♦ Add tomato sauce, spices and ½ c. of broth.

♦ Bring to a boil and simmer additional 2 – 3 minutes – chicken and peppers should be fully cooked at this time.

♦ Stir cornstarch and water together until smooth.

♦ Slowly pour into boiling liquid stirring constantly until thickened to medium consistency. You may not need all the cornstarch mix. If too thick add more chicken broth.

♦ Served with rice.

Black pepper comes from dried green pepper corn. White pepper is the matured pepper corn. Black pepper has a less biting taste than the white pepper. In the United States white pepper's primary use is in white colored sauces where dark specks are undesirable.

Recipe Notes

_____

_____

_____

_____

_____

_____

_____

_____

_____

_____

_____

_____

_____

_____

_____

_____

Chicken Etouffee

4 (6 oz.)	chicken breast – ½" diced raw
2 TBSP.	butter
1 c.	celery – ¼" diced
1 c.	green pepper – ¼" diced
1 TBSP.	crushed garlic
2 tsp.	salt
2 TBSP.	tomato paste
1 tsp.	cayenne pepper
12	green onions – ½" cuts
1 TBSP.	cornstarch
2 TBSP.	cold water

Method:

♦ Heat butter in large skillet until bubbly.

♦ Add celery, peppers, onions, garlic and spices. Sauté five minutes or until all vegetables are soft cooked.

♦ Add raw diced chicken and tomato paste. Simmer in skillet for 15 minutes – covered. Stir occasionally.

♦ At this point check mixture; if runny with liquid add mixed cornstarch and water to skillet to thicken to medium consistency.

♦ Served with rice.

Tellicherry black pepper from India is considered the finest quality pepper. The tellicherry peppercorn is twice the size of a normal peppercorn and contains three times the spice oil.

Recipe Notes

_____
_____
_____
_____
_____
_____
_____
_____
_____
_____
_____
_____
_____
_____
_____

Mardi Gras Chicken

4 (6 oz.)	chicken breast - – ¼" strips
1 TBSP.	butter
1 TBSP.	vegetable oil
6	green onions - – ½" cuts
1 c.	cut okra (Canned is fine)
2 c.	diced ripe tomatoes
1 tsp.	thyme
1 tsp.	cayenne pepper
2 tsp.	salt

Method:

♦ Heat butter and oil in large skillet until medium hot.

♦ Sauté chicken strips for 3 – 4 minutes. Remove from skillet.

♦ Add onions, okra and tomatoes to the skillet. Sauté five minutes – until tomatoes soften and form juice. Add spices and salt.

♦ Return chicken to skillet, coating each strip with sauce.

♦ Cover and simmer for 10 – 12 minutes at low heat.

♦ Serve

Italian

Who doesn't like Italian? In most surveys it is the most popular choice of the American public. Italian dishes are part of every Zehnder family celebration. For those of you who have a copy of my first cookbook you already know that my Great Uncle was an Italian chef. The Zehnder family treats his recipes like heirloom jewels.

Italian dishes incorporate olive oil, tomatoes, garlic and spices, usually oregano. In most recipes today, there is a "one sauce fits all" mentality. As any good Italian cook knows, there are many tomato sauces. Each sauce has its own taste and character. My favorite story concerning Italian sauce is the tradition behind Putenesca sauce. Legend has it that Putenesca was first made by "ladies of the evening" during the 17th century. The pungent aroma of this sauce, it was said, was used to lure men to the red light districts of Florence. True or not, it's an interesting story.

Olive oil, used for thousands of years for cooking, heating, and lighting homes. Why is it then that very few people know about olive oil? Extra virgin, virgin, olive oil, and pomace are all terms used when referring to olive oil. Each term tells you something about the oil and how it was produced. I'll try to explain, in general terms, what they all mean and why some oils cost more than others.

Recipe Notes

_____

_____

_____

_____

_____

_____

_____

_____

_____

_____

_____

_____

_____

_____

_____

_____

Chicken Parmigiani

4 (6 oz.)	chicken breast		1 c.	dry red wine (opt.)
3	eggs		¼ tsp.	oregano
½ c.	milk		½ tsp.	crushed garlic
1 ½ c.	dry bread crumbs seasoned		1 ½ tsp.	butter
¾ c.	olive oil		½ c.	grated parmesan
3 c.	tomato sauce		4 slices	mozzarella cheese
½ tsp.	basil			

Method:

♦ Rinse breast under cold water.

♦ Lay breasts on wood cutting board and pound with side of knife blade until about a quarter inch thick.

♦ Mix eggs and milk with fork until blended.

♦ Dip breast in egg milk mixture then press firmly into dry crumbs.

♦ Heat olive oil in skillet to medium heat – brown chicken breasts on both sides.

♦ Remove from skillet, drain remaining oil and place breasts in shallow Corningware dish.

♦ Return skillet to heat and add sauce, basil, oregano and garlic.

♦ Heat to boiling – simmer 10 minutes – stir in butter and wine.

♦ Pour sauce over chicken, sprinkle with parmesan and place in 350° oven covered for 25 minutes.

♦ Uncover and top with mozzarella.

♦ Return to oven for 10 minutes or until cheese melts.

Extra virgin olive oil comes from the first pressing of the olives. Gently squeezed, like fine grapes, the "run off" oil is fragrant, thick, and green in color. Most expensive of all the olive oils, it imparts flavors and aromas to foods cooked in it. This is the finest oil for salad dressings. if you use olive oil in the place of butter on your breads and rolls use extra virgin.

Recipe Notes

_____

_____

_____

_____

_____

_____

_____

_____

_____

_____

_____

_____

_____

_____

_____

Chicken Alfredo

4 (6oz)	chicken breast	3 oz.	butter
¼ c.	butter	3 oz.	all purpose flour
¼ c.	olive oil	3 tsp.	salt
1 c.	mushrooms – sliced ¼" thick	1 tsp.	black pepper ground
¼ c.	diced Spanish onion	2 c.	milk
¼ c.	grated parmesan cheese		

Method:

♦ Heat olive oil in large skillet until medium hot (325°)

♦ Add butter and stir until butter melts.

♦ Rinse breast and brown on both sides – remove from skillet.

♦ Add mushrooms and onions to skillet and sauté until tender (3 – 4 minutes). Remove from heat.

♦ In a separate saucepan melt 3-oz. butter. Stir in the flour, salt and pepper. Continue heating at low heat, stirring constantly, until mixture is smooth and bubbly.

♦ Pour in milk, increase heat to medium, and stir until thick **– Careful!** Don't scorch the pan! The mixture will just begin to boil when ready.

♦ Stir in parmesan – taste for salt and pepper.

♦ Place chicken breast on top of mushrooms- onions and pour over the Alfredo sauce.

♦ Simmer at low heat, covered, for 20 – 25 minutes until breast are tender.

♦ Serve.

Cardamon is a spice which has been used for over 2000 years. Native to India, cardamon is used throughout Europe and Asia primarily in baking. Blended with coffee beans, it is a popular beverage in the Mideast.

Recipe Notes

_____
_____
_____
_____
_____
_____
_____
_____
_____
_____
_____
_____
_____
_____
_____
_____

Chicken Tetrazzini

¼ c.	butter	½ lb.	spaghetti
¼ c.	all purpose flour	8 oz.	canned mushrooms
1 c.	milk	3 c.	diced cooked chicken
1 c.	chicken stock		breast
	or bouillon	½ c.	grated parmesan
½ tsp.	salt	½ tsp.	pepper ground
¾ c.	cream		

Method:

♦ In a saucepan heat the butter until melted and stir in the flour.

♦ Heat at low temperature, stirring constantly, until smooth and thick.

♦ Add milk and stock; heat until thickened at medium heat, stirring regularly. Add salt and pepper, stir in cream.

♦ Cook spaghetti and drain.

♦ Mix half sauce with mushrooms and spaghetti.

♦ Add diced cooked chicken and remaining sauce.

♦ Mix well until chicken is spread throughout mix.

♦ Pour into medium deep baking pan.

♦ Sprinkle with parmesan.

♦ Bake at 350° for 30 minutes.

Once pressed, the olive mash is stirred and re-pressed. The juices of this pressing contain both liquid and oil. Since oil is lighter than water, the floating oil is skimmed off. This is virgin olive oil so called because no heat has been applied to it. Virgin oil is less expensive than extra virgin, and is a good choice for sautéing where strong flavors are introduced to it such as onions or garlic. Very good as an oil for making salad dressings.

Recipe Notes

_____

_____

_____

_____

_____

_____

_____

_____

_____

_____

_____

_____

_____

_____

_____

Chicken Putenesca

¼ c.	olive oil	2 tsp.	salt
½ TBSP.	chopped garlic	2 tsp.	pepper
1 c.	diced onion	1 c.	slices black olives
3 c.	canned tomatoes w/ juice		drained
6 oz	tomato sauce	3	anchovy fillets canned
2 tsp.	oregano	½ c.	olive oil
2	bay leaves	4 (6 oz.)	chicken breasts
1 c.	dry red wine		

Method:

♦ Add olive oil to large saucepan and heat to medium hot.

♦ Add garlic and onions. Sauté 3 – 4 minutes or until onions are soft.

♦ Stir in tomatoes, sauce, spices and salt and pepper.

♦ Bring to boil, then turn down to medium heat and simmer for 1½ hours.

♦ Add olives, anchovies and red wine.

♦ Simmer 15 minutes. Set aside.

♦ In a skillet heat ½ cup olive oil to medium hot.

♦ Rinse chicken breasts and sauté in oil until brown on both sides.

♦ Drain remaining oil from skillet and pour sauce over chicken breasts.

   Simmer 20 minutes or until done.

♦ Serve breasts in sauce over pasta.

Olive oil is the product of cooked olive mash. After the second cold pressing of the olives, heat is applied and the olive mash is brought to a boil. The liquid/oil is drained off and the resulting oil is called olive oil. Slightly bitter with a sharper olive taste, use this oil as only a minor product in the recipe or when heavy flavors such as tomatoes are added. Not a good choice for salad dressings.

Recipe Notes

_____
_____
_____
_____
_____
_____
_____
_____
_____
_____
_____
_____
_____
_____
_____
_____

Chicken Tomato Basil Sauce

12 oz.	tomato sauce	½ c.	olive oil
2 tsp.	salt	1 ½ c.	all purpose flour
1 tsp.	black pepper ground	4 (6 oz.)	chicken breasts
1 tsp.	garlic salt		
1 TBSP.	fresh chopped basil		

Method:

♦ Heat tomato sauce to bubbling in saucepan.

♦ Add salt, pepper and garlic salt. Set aside.

♦ Heat olive oil in large skillet to medium hot.

♦ Rinse chicken breasts in cool water, pat dry.

♦ Place flour in plastic storage bag – add breasts, one at a time and coat with flour.

♦ Sauté breasts in olive oil until brown on both sides. Remove from heat.

♦ Drain excess olive oil.

♦ Add fresh basil to sauce – return to medium heat for five minutes. Basil is best when added at the end of cooking.

♦ Pour over breasts in skillet – return to stove.

♦ Simmer breasts in sauce for 15 to 20 minutes or until done and tender.

♦ Serve.

The olive mash goes through one more process before it's discarded. Pomace is the result of adding chemicals to the olive mash, extracting all remaining oil. Cheapest of all the olive oils. Pomace is not an acceptable cooking oil. In Europe and the Mideast pomace is used for lamp oil. Even if it was acceptable for cooking I would still question the chemical process used to extract the oil and any possible health ramifications.

Recipe Notes

_____

_____

_____

_____

_____

_____

_____

_____

_____

_____

_____

_____

_____

_____

_____

Chicken Cacciatore

½ c.	olive oil	4 oz.	tomato sauce
2	green peppers - ½" strips	1 tsp.	oregano
2	red peppers - ½" strips	1 tsp.	marjoram
1	onion - ½" strips	1 c.	dry red wine
2 tsp.	garlic chopped	½ c.	olive oil
2 tsp.	salt	1 ½ c.	all purpose flour
2 tsp.	pepper	6 (6 oz.)	chicken breasts
24 oz.	diced canned tomatoes	½ lb.	angel-hair pasta

Method:

♦ Heat oil in large saucepan to medium hot. Add peppers and onions – sauté until soft.

♦ Add garlic, salt and pepper. Sauté 2 minutes.

♦ Pour in tomatoes, sauce and spices. Simmer 1-½ hours.

♦ Pour in red wine and simmer an additional 20 minutes.

♦ Heat olive oil to medium hot in large skillet.

♦ Place flour in plastic storage bag. Drop breasts, one at a time, dusting each breast evenly.

♦ Sauté breasts in olive oil until browned on both sides.

♦ Place browned breasts in deep baking dish. Pour sauce over breasts – cover and bake 30 minutes at 325°.

♦ Serve breast in sauce over angel-hair pasta.

Garlic was a favorite of the Egyptian Pharoahs. Prized for its intense flavor, many other cultures adapted their cooking styles to include garlic. Roman soldiers ate garlic believing it gave strength and courage. Although popular in modern Greek dishes, garlic was seldom used by the ancient Greeks. Recent medical studies have shown the consumption of garlic helps in the prevention of heart disease.

Recipe Notes

_____

_____

_____

_____

_____

_____

_____

_____

_____

_____

_____

_____

_____

_____

_____

_____

Chicken Verde

2 TBSP.	chopped green onions	2 TBSP.	lemon juice
2 tsp.	chopped garlic	1/3 c.	olive oil
2 TBSP.	capers – rinsed	2 tsp.	salt
3 TBSP.	chopped parsley	1 tsp.	black pepper ground
4 (6oz.)	chicken breasts	¼ c.	olive oil

Method:

♦ Place all ingredients except breasts and ¼ cup olive oil, in mixing bowl and blend well.

♦ Rinse breasts and pat dry.

♦ Brush breasts with olive oil and place on broiler tray. Have broiler set on medium heat.

♦ Broil breasts on low rack of broiler, flipping breasts so both sides are browned.

♦ When breasts are done, (10 – 12) minutes, Spoon equal portions of Verde on each breast, spreading evenly across each breast.

♦ Return to broiler for 2 – 3 minutes – until onions and parsley just begin to brown.

♦ Serve topped breast with warm garlic bread slices.

Fennel, probably the oldest cultivated spice, was used throughout the ancient world as a "cure all" medicine. Modern Italians blend fennel into sausage and tomato sauces. Strong and distinct, fennel imports a sweet taste when cooked.

Recipe Notes

_____
_____
_____
_____
_____
_____
_____
_____
_____
_____
_____
_____
_____
_____
_____

Chicken Florentine

1 lb.	fresh spinach	2 tsp.	oregano
½ c.	water	2 tsp.	garlic salt
2 tsp.	salt	1 tsp.	basil
1 tsp.	black pepper ground	½ c.	olive oil
½ c.	grated parmesan	4 (6 oz.)	chicken breasts
½ c.	cream		

Method:

♦ Wash spinach and remove coarse stems.

♦ Place in saucepan, add water, salt and pepper.

♦ Cover and bring to medium heat for 15 minutes.

♦ Remove from heat and drain excess liquid.

♦ Set aside – off heat but covered.

♦ Mix spices and garlic salt – this is your seasoning.

♦ Rinse breasts and pat dry.

♦ Lightly rub breasts on both sides with seasonings.

♦ Place oil in skillet and heat to medium hot.

♦ Brown seasoned breast on both sides.

♦ Place breasts in deep baking dish.

♦ Put spinach on top of breasts.

♦ Pour cream over spinach and sprinkle with parmesan.

♦ Cover and bake at 325° for 30 minutes.

Oregano and majoram are cousins. Similar in flavor, many cultures have used these two spices interchangeably. Both are perennials, coming up year after year. If you're planning an herb garden, these two are easy to grow and will provide you with enough to share with friends.

Recipe Notes

_____

_____

_____

_____

_____

_____

_____

_____

_____

_____

_____

_____

_____

_____

_____

_____

Chicken Marsala

4 (6 oz.)	chicken breasts		2 TBSP.	butter
1 tsp.	salt		3 TBSP.	olive oil
1 tsp.	black pepper ground		½ c.	dry marsala wine
1 ½ c.	all purpose flour		½ c.	chicken broth
2 TBSP.	soft butter			

Method:

♦ Flatten each breast to ¼" thick. Cut each breast into 4 pieces. Lightly season each piece with salt and pepper.

♦ Dip in flour, shake off excess flour.

♦ Heat 2 TBSP. butter and 3 TBSP. olive oil to medium hot in large skillet.

♦ Brown off flour breast pieces in butter and olive oil.

♦ Remove breasts pieces from skillet and drain excess oil.

♦ Pour marsala wine into skillet and gently scrape browned crumbs from bottom of skillet.

♦ Add chicken broth and continue simmering until almost all crumbs are dissolved.

♦ Stir in softened butter and simmer until liquid is reduced by 1/3.

♦ Return breast to skillet and spoon sauce over chicken. Simmer additional five minutes or until breasts are tender.

♦ Serve.

Basil is a delicate herb. Best in its fresh form, basil should be added toward the end of any cooking procedure. Store basil in a cool place. Fresh basil will turn black below 40 degrees so don't refrigerate.

Recipe Notes

_____

_____

_____

_____

_____

_____

_____

_____

_____

_____

_____

_____

_____

_____

_____

Chicken Pizzaiola

3 TBSP.	olive oil	2	bay leaves
1 c.	diced onions	2 tsp.	salt
½ TBSP.	chopped garlic	1 tsp.	black pepper ground
4 c.	diced tomatoes	½ c.	olive oil
1	6 oz. can tomato paste	1 ½ c.	all purpose flour
3 tsp.	oregano	6 (6 oz.)	chicken breasts
3 tsp.	basil		

Method:

◆ Heat 3-TBSP. olive oil to medium hot in large saucepan.

◆ Sauté onions in oil until soft. Add garlic and continue to sauté 2 minutes more.

◆ Add diced tomatoes, paste, spices, salt and pepper.

◆ Stir until mixed and simmer for one hour, stirring occasionally.

◆ Taste for salt and pepper – add more if you desire.

◆ Heat half-cup oil in skillet to medium hot.

◆ Place flour in plastic storage bag and add breasts, one at a time, dusting each evenly.

◆ Sauté breasts in skillet, browning on both sides.

◆ Drain excess oil.

◆ Pour sauce over breasts in skillet and simmer for twenty minutes or until tender.

◆ Serve.

French

France! Need I say more? A cuisine that dates back to the middle ages. Centuries of culinary tradition and an almost fanatical reverence toward food makes France the fine dining center of the world.

What differentiates French cooking is its liberal use of butter and wine. The average Frenchman consumes twice the amount of butter than his American counterpart, yet heart disease is half that of the United States. It's believed that red wine consumption by the French is responsible for this French Paradox.

In addition to butter and wine, the French love their shallots and cheese. I've incorporated all of these features into the French recipes that follow.

FRANCE

CORSICA

Classic herb combinations give dishes a unique signature taste. Three famous and popular herb combinations are bouquet garni, fine herbs, and herbs de Province. Used extensively in commercial cooking, these spice mixtures also have many great applications for the amateur culinary enthusiast.

Recipe Notes

_____

_____

_____

_____

_____

_____

_____

_____

_____

_____

_____

_____

_____

_____

_____

_____

Coq Au Vin

4 (6oz.)	chicken breast
1 c.	all purpose flour
3 TBSP.	butter
½ c.	lean diced ham
1 ½ c.	tomato juice
½ c.	dry white wine
1 c.	canned mushroom pieces – drained
2 tsp.	chopped garlic
1 tsp.	black ground pepper
1	bay leaves
1 tsp.	thyme
1 c.	chopped onion

Method:

♦ Heat butter to medium in large skillet.

♦ Coat chicken in flour and sauté in butter 2 – 3 minutes. Remove from skillet.

♦ Place chicken in deep casserole dish. Sprinkle diced ham on chicken.

♦ In the same skillet add all remaining ingredients and bring to a boil, stirring to bring up browned bits from surface of the skillet.

♦ Pour over the chicken and ham.

♦ Cover and bake at 350° for twenty minutes.

♦ Serve.

Soups, stews, broths, and French sauces. What do they have in common? BOUQUET GARNI. Bouquet garni is parsley, thyme, and bay leaves all tied-up in a cheesecloth bag. Occasionally other spices are added to this bag of spices which is lowered into boiling soups and stocks. Wrapping the spices in cheesecloth allows you to determine how strong a spice flavor you want. Just pull it out at any point in the cooking process.

Recipe Notes

_____
_____
_____
_____
_____
_____
_____
_____
_____
_____
_____
_____
_____
_____

Chicken Parisienne

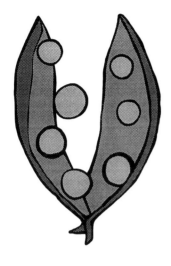

3 (6 oz.)	chicken breast – ½" diced
1 TBSP.	butter
1 TBSP.	vegetable oil
1 ½ c.	canned whole onions – drained
1 ½ c.	chicken broth
2 tsp.	salt
½ tsp.	thyme
½ tsp.	black pepper ground
1 ½ c.	frozen or fresh peas
2 c.	cooked medium noodles - drained
1 ½ c.	grated gruyere cheese

Method:

♦ Sauté diced raw chicken in butter and oil 2 – 3 minutes.

♦ Add onions and sauté until hot 2 – 3 minutes.

♦ Pour in chicken broth and stir to bring up browned bits from surface of skillet.

♦ Add salt and spices.

♦ Next put peas into skillet and heat until peas are tender.

♦ Toss in drained / cooked noodles and mix all ingredients together.

♦ When hot, serve sprinkled with cheese.

Fine herbs consist of equal parts of parsley, tarragon, chives, and chervil. A classic French seasoning for eggs, soft cheese and herb butters drizzled over vegetables or fish.

Recipe Notes

_____

_____

_____

_____

_____

_____

_____

_____

_____

_____

_____

_____

_____

_____

Chicken with White Wine and Mushrooms

4 (6 oz.)	chicken breast
2 TBSP.	butter
1 TBSP.	vegetable oil
2 c.	sliced raw mushrooms
½ c.	diced onions
3 c.	chicken broth
¾ c.	dry white wine
2 c.	converted rice
1	bay leaves
½ tsp.	black pepper ground
2 tsp.	salt

Method:

♦ Sauté chicken breasts in butter oil, 2 –3 minutes.

♦ Remove from skillet and place in large casserole dish.

♦ Add mushrooms and onions to skillet. Sauté for 2 – 3 minutes.

♦ Pour in broth and wine. Bring to boil, stirring up any browned bits from surface of skillet.

♦ Add rice, spices and salt. Bring to boil.

♦ Pour mixture over chicken breasts in casserole dish.

♦ Cover and bake 45 minutes at 325°.

♦ Serve.

Herbs de Province-a natural combination of spices to season grilled meats and poultry. Rosemary's a must along with bay leaf, thyme, basil, and savory. This mixture is a dried spice mix-not fresh. This is my personal favorite on lamb chops.

Recipe Notes

_____

_____

_____

_____

_____

_____

_____

_____

_____

_____

_____

_____

_____

_____

Chicken au Poivre

4 (6oz.)	chicken breasts
2 tsp.	salt
2 TBSP.	cracked black pepper
2 TBSP.	butter
1 TBSP.	vegetable oil
¼ c.	cognac
1 ½ c.	chicken broth
2 TBSP.	cornstarch
2 TBSP.	cold water
1 TBSP.	chopped parsley
2 TBSP.	hard butter

Method:

♦ Wash chicken under running cold water. Leave damp.

♦ Place pepper and salt on large platter. Press chicken into salt and pepper. Coating each piece evenly on both sides.

♦ Heat butter and oil in large skillet. Add chicken and sauté 3 – 4 minutes on each side – until done. Remove from skillet and keep hot.

♦ Pour cognac into skillet stir to release any browned pieces on surface of skillet.

♦ Add chicken broth. Bring to boil.

♦ Stir cornstarch and water together. Add to boiling broth to lightly thicken.

♦ Toss in parsley. Break butter into ½" pieces and whisk into broth until melted.

♦ Place peppered chicken on platter. Pour sauce over chicken.

♦ Serve.

Chervil or French parsley has no apparent link to sorcery or folklore. Used in cooking for 2000 years chervil imparts a mild anise taste, and is usually combined with a variety of other spices. Widely used in French cooking, chervil is relatively unknown in America. A great seasoning addition to potato salad!

Recipe Notes

_____

_____

_____

_____

_____

_____

_____

_____

_____

_____

_____

_____

_____

_____

_____

Chicken Mornay

½ c.	butter
½ c.	all purpose flour
3 c.	milk
2 TBSP.	dry sherry
2 tsp.	capers
3 (6oz.)	chicken breasts – ½" diced cooked
2 tsp.	salt
1 tsp.	black pepper ground
½ lb.	cooked medium noodles – drained
½ c.	grated parmesan cheese

Method:

♦ Add butter to saucepan and heat to bubbly.

♦ Stir in flour with wire whip – allow mixture to soften – mix well.

♦ Pour in milk and heat at medium heat, whisking with wire whip to avoid burning, should be gravy-like consistency – add milk if too thick.

♦ When thickened, add capers and sherry.

♦ Place cooked noodles on bottom of casserole dish.

♦ Top with diced chicken season with salt and pepper.

♦ Pour over the mornay sauce, jiggle dish so sauce works its way down through the chicken and noodles.

♦ Sprinkle with cheese and cover dish.

♦ Bake at 350° for 20 minutes.

♦ Serve.

Often used but rarely eaten. Parsley is one of the most widely used herbs in the world. In the United States we use it primarily as a garnish while the French and Italians love its flavor in many dishes. Cultivated for thousands of years, parsley was a favorite of the Roman Empire. Parsley crowns topped the head of the special guests at the emperor's banquets. Nobles ate parsley to freshen their breath after dinner. In England when a child asks where he came from the common response is "From the parsley patch" not from the stork..

Recipe Notes

Chicken Boivin

6	thin skinned potatoes
2 TBSP.	vegetable oil
1 TBSP.	butter
1 c.	canned artichoke hearts
1 c.	large onion diced
4 (6oz.)	chicken breasts – ½" strips
1 TBSP.	butter
1 TBSP.	vegetable oil
2 tsp.	salt
1 tsp.	thyme
1 tsp.	black pepper ground

Method:

♦ Using a melon baller cut small balls out of the potatoes – do not peel.

♦ Heat oil and butter in skillet to medium heat.

♦ Cover and sauté potato balls 5 – 6 minutes, shaking pan on burner to keep potatoes from sticking.

♦ Add onions and artichoke hearts. Cover and continue to sauté 3 – 4 minutes. Potatoes should be soft but not breaking apart at this point. You may need to add a tablespoon of butter.

♦ In a separate skillet sauté the chicken 3 – 4 minutes. Halfway through sautéing season with spices, salt and pepper.

♦ Remove chicken from skillet. Mix with potatoes, artichoke and onions. Cover and sauté 1 – 2 minutes.

♦ Remove from skillet and serve.

Infused oils are cooking or salad oils that have a distinct spice / herb taste. You achieve this flavor by placing fresh herbs / spices in room temperature and allow the oil to absorb the spice flavor. A few hours will give you a mild flavor while several days provides a strong taste. Like compound butters, infused oils help to carry the spice flavor throughout the dish you're preparing. It is, therefore, necessary to use only the best fresh spices / herbs since your final product will noticably taste like the spices used.

Recipe Notes

_____

_____

_____

_____

_____

_____

_____

_____

_____

_____

_____

_____

_____

_____

Chicken with Madeira and Onions

3 TBSP.	butter
1 TBSP.	vegetable oil
4 (6oz.)	chicken breasts
1 c.	fresh mushrooms – sliced
1 c.	onions – diced
3 TBSP.	all purpose flour
2 c.	Madeira wine
1 c.	chicken broth
1 tsp.	thyme
1 tsp.	black pepper ground
1 tsp.	salt

Method:

♦ Heat butter and oil to medium heat in large skillet.

♦ Brown chicken breasts 2 – 3 minutes on each side. Remove from skillet.

♦ Add onions and mushrooms to skillet. Sauté 3 – 4 minutes.

♦ Whisk flour into mushrooms and onions until smooth.

♦ Add all remaining ingredients except chicken.

♦ Bring to boil, whisking constantly.

♦ Return chicken to sauce in skillet.

♦ Cover and simmer for 15 minutes – until done

♦ Serve.

Saffron is the world's most expensive spice. One acre produces one pound of saffron and must be hand picked. Each flower has three stigmas. Saffron is the dried stigma thread. Just a few threads of saffron are needed to season a dish.

Recipe Notes

_____

_____

_____

_____

_____

_____

_____

_____

_____

_____

_____

_____

_____

_____

Chicken with Red Wine and Shallots

1 c.	dry red wine
2 TBSP.	butter
½ c.	split shallots (small whole onions)
¼ c.	water
2 tsp.	salt
2 tsp.	oregano
1 TBSP.	brown sugar
4 (6oz.)	chicken breasts – raw

Method:

♦ Place chicken breasts in large casserole dish.

♦ Combine all remaining ingredients and heat to boiling in a small

saucepan.

♦ Pour over raw breasts. Cover casserole.

♦ Bake at 350° for 35 minutes or until chicken is done.

♦ Serve with rice pilaf.

A few sprigs of rosemary, a half dozen tarragon leaves, or three medium size basil leaves will season two cups of oil. The oil can be olive, soy, canola or any other liquid oil. Remember that the spices will continue to flavor the oil as long as it remains in it. Remove the spices when your desired taste is reached. Always use whole spices and herbs so that they are easily removed. This infused oil will last several weeks under refrigeration.

Recipe Notes

_____

_____

_____

_____

_____

_____

_____

_____

_____

_____

_____

_____

_____

_____

Chicken with Brie Sauce

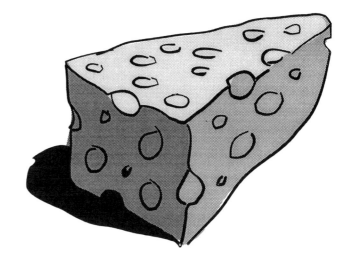

4 (6oz.)	chicken breasts
2 TBSP.	butter
1 TBSP.	vegetable oil
1/3 c.	all purpose flour
1/3c.	butter
3 c.	milk
2 tsp.	salt
½ tsp.	white pepper ground
6 oz.	brie cheese
1 TBSP.	chopped parsley

Method:

♦ Sauté chicken in butter and oil in large skillet for 2 – 3 minutes. Remove from skillet.

♦ Place 1/3-cup butter in same skillet and heat to bubbly.

♦ Whisk in flour with wire whip at medium heat until mixture is smooth 2 – 3 minutes.

♦ Pour in milk and heat until thicken – whisking constantly.

♦ Add salt, pepper and Brie cheese that was been cut into small pieces.

♦ Whisk at medium low heat until cheese is melted.

♦ Return breasts to skillet, and simmer in cheese sauce for 5 – 6 minutes or until chicken is done.

♦ Remove from skillet, ladle extra sauce on chicken, and sprinkle with chopped parsley and serve.

Rosemary is a fragrant spice that closely resembles pine needles. In Shakespeare's day, bouquets of rosemary were a sign of love, much like a bouquet of roses is today. Rosemary compliments both poultry and seafood.

Recipe Notes

Chicken Royal

4 (6oz.)	chicken breasts
2 TBSP.	butter
1 TBSP.	vegetable oil
½ c.	dry red wine
1 TBSP.	brown sugar
2 tsp.	salt
2 c.	ripe tomatoes – diced
½ c.	ripe olives – sliced
1 tsp.	thyme
½ tsp.	black pepper – ground

Method:

♦ Sauté chicken breasts in butter and oil in a large skillet 2 – 3 minutes – remove from skillet.

♦ Pour in wine and stir around bottom of skillet to loosen any browned crumbs.

♦ Add brown sugar and salt. Mix well with wine.

♦ Place tomatoes, olives and spices in wine.

♦ Sauté 2 – 3 minutes – tomatoes will soften and form a liquid.

♦ Place chicken back into skillet with tomato - olive sauce.

♦ Cover and simmer 5 – 6 minutes – until chicken is done.

♦ Serve.

Californian

California Cuisine is food gone wild!   The creative minds of California chefs amaze me!

Fruits, avocados, zucchini, olives and olive oil make California foods a category all their own.

California is just about the only place where you rarely see butter served with rolls or bread. The norm for restaurants is flavored olive oils. With so many fresh foods readily available, is it any wonder that California frequently is the trendsetter for the rest of the country?

Several new oils have come on the market over the past five years, primarily cooking oils. These new products blend themselves well to new cooking techniques. Rapeseed, grapeseed, and avocado, are examples of new age oil. Heat resistant and versatile, these oils will see increased use over the next few years.

Recipe Notes

_____

_____

_____

_____

_____

_____

_____

_____

_____

_____

_____

_____

_____

_____

_____

Chicken in Strawberry Sauce

3 c.   ripe strawberries
1 ½ c.   sugar
¼ tsp.   ground ginger
2 TBSP.   cornstarch
3 TBSP.   cold water
4 (6oz.)   chicken breasts
1 TBSP.   butter
1 TBSP.   vegetable oil
1 tsp.   salt

Method:

♦ Wash and hull strawberries. Cut in half to make three cups.

♦ Place strawberries, sugar and ginger in saucepan and slowly heat to medium. Crush half the strawberries while cooking to make juice. Bring to boil, stirring constantly.

♦ Mix cornstarch and cold water. Add slowly to boiling strawberries until a syrup consistency achieved. You may not need all cornstarch mix. Set aside off heat.

♦ Heat butter and oil in a large skillet until medium hot. Sauté chicken 3 – 4 minutes on each side – until done.

♦ Remove from skillet. Drain on paper towels.

♦ Ladle sauce over chicken and serve.

Rapeseed oil has been around for a long time but few people took advantage of it. Enter the country of Canada, who saw rapeseed growing in harsh climates with short growing seasons. With the price of cooking oils at an all time high, Canada aggressively began growing rapeseed and processing oil. Rapeseed's name, not very appealing, was changed to canola. Canola oil contains less saturated fat than most other oils and is excellent for cooking. It's rapidly becoming a preferred use oil.

Recipe Notes

_____
_____
_____
_____
_____
_____
_____
_____
_____
_____
_____
_____
_____
_____
_____
_____

Chinatown
Stir-fry Chicken with Zucchini and Summer Squash

3 (6oz.)	chicken breasts – ¼" strips
1 tsp.	salt
1 tsp.	black pepper, ground
1 TBSP.	vegetable oil
2 c.	zucchini – ¼" strips
1 c.	summer squash – ¼" strips
1 TBSP.	vegetable oil
2 tsp.	sesame oil

Method:

♦ Heat wok to high heat. Add oil.

♦ Quickly add chicken, salt and pepper to wok and stir-fry 2 – 3 minutes. Remove from wok. Drain oil and liquid.

♦ Reheat wok to high heat. Add oil

♦ Immediately add zucchini and summer squash. Stir-fry 2 – 3 minutes – squash will be slightly limp but crunchy.

♦ Add chicken to squash in wok. Add sesame oil.

♦ Toss one minute until all ingredients hot.

♦ Serve.

"Sponge oil" pick-up predominant flavors in a recipe and disburses that flavor throughout the dish. Avocado is one of these sponge oils used selectively in recipes that require intense flavor, avocado oil is a great addition to the kitchen cupboard. A smoke point of 425, this oil is a great choice for high heat cooking. Get a bottle and play with it, you'll be surprised at the results.

Recipe Notes

_____
_____
_____
_____
_____
_____
_____
_____
_____
_____
_____
_____
_____
_____

San Diego Chicken

4 (6oz.)	chicken breasts – ½" strips
1 tsp.	cayenne pepper
½ tsp.	cilantro
½ tsp.	cumin
½ tsp.	salt
2 TBSP.	corn oil
2	green peppers – ½" slices
1	red pepper – ½" slices
4	green onions
1	soft (not fully ripe) avocado – ½" slices
8	flour tortillas

Method:

♦ Toss chicken strips with spices and salt. Allow to set for 20 minutes.

♦ Heat oil in large skillet to medium hot. Add seasoned chicken strips and sauté 3 – 4 minutes.

♦ Add peppers and onions to skillet with chicken. Sauté 2 –3 minutes.

♦ Toss in avocado slices and sauté 1 –2 minutes – until avocados are hot.

♦ Heat tortillas on a non-oiled skillet at medium heat 30 – 45 seconds on each side.

♦ Fill center of tortilla with fajita mix.

♦ Serve with salsa and sour cream.

Pink peppercorns, the "spice of the 90's", is not really pepper. This small dry berry from Asia is noted for its unique sweet/hot flavor and unusual color presentation. Pink peppercorns compliment both poultry and fish.

Recipe Notes

_____

_____

_____

_____

_____

_____

_____

_____

_____

_____

_____

_____

_____

Napa Valley Chicken

4 (6oz.)	chicken breasts
2 TBSP.	vegetable oil
½ c.	diced onions
1 tsp.	salt
1 tsp.	black pepper ground
2 c.	converted rice
3 ½ c.	chicken broth – hot
½ c.	dry white wine

Method:

♦ Heat oil in large skillet to medium heat.

♦ Sauté chicken 2 – 3 minutes on each side. Remove from skillet.

♦ In a large baking dish place uncooked rice, broth, onions, salt, pepper and wine.

♦ Place partially cooked chicken on top of mixture. Chicken will be in liquid.

♦ Cover and bake at 350° for 45 minutes or until rice is soft.

♦ Serve.

Juniper berries, the poor man's spice, was used widely throughout the Middle Ages. Readily available to all and free for the picking, juniper berries was the main spice to prince and pauper. The popularity of wild game has brought a renaissance to this forgotten berry.

Recipe Notes

_____

_____

_____

_____

_____

_____

_____

_____

_____

_____

_____

_____

_____

_____

_____

Chicken in Monterey Crab Sauce

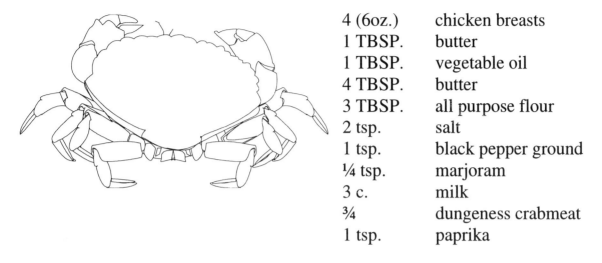

4 (6oz.)	chicken breasts
1 TBSP.	butter
1 TBSP.	vegetable oil
4 TBSP.	butter
3 TBSP.	all purpose flour
2 tsp.	salt
1 tsp.	black pepper ground
¼ tsp.	marjoram
3 c.	milk
¾	dungeness crabmeat
1 tsp.	paprika

Method:

♦ Heat butter and oil in skillet and heat to medium heat.

♦ Sauté chicken for 2 – 3 minutes. Remove from skillet. Drain skillet of oil and liquid.

♦ Place butter in skillet and heat to bubbly. Stir in flour, cook until soft and smooth.

♦ Pour in milk and add salt and spices. Bring to medium heat, stirring constantly until smooth and thickened like gravy.

♦ Add crabmeat and stir in. Remove from heat.

♦ Place chicken in baking dish – pour sauce over chicken.

♦ Cover and bake at 325° for 25 – 30 minutes.

♦ Serve.

Caribbean

St. Thomas, Jamaica, Antiqua and Trinidad. Cruise ships on the horizon and crystal clear waters. This is the Caribbean that many of us think about on those icy cold days of winter.

Each of the Islands has developed its own special foods. Cuban black bean dishes, chutneys, and curries are all part of this tropical cuisine.

Over the past few years many chefs have begun to examine Caribbean foods. Some even say that it is soon to become the next "hot trend"! Whatever happens, I'm sure you'll enjoy the variety of tastes offered in this section.

Cuba

Curry powder, like chili powder, is a blend of many spices including cumin. Curries are classified as sweet or hot. Introduced to western culture by way of British soldiers stationed in India, curry powders continue to grow in popularity.

Recipe Notes

_____

_____

_____

_____

_____

_____

_____

_____

_____

_____

_____

_____

_____

_____

_____

_____

Trinidad Curry Chicken

2 TBSP.	vegetable oil	3	green peppers – ¼" strips
4 (6oz.)	chicken breasts	2	carrots – ¼" strips
1 c.	chicken broth	½ c.	unsweetened coconut
1 c.	chablis wine		cream
2 TBSP.	curry powder	½ c.	shredded coconut
1 TBSP.	salt	3 TBSP.	cornstarch
2 tsp.	black pepper ground	4 TBSP.	cold water

Method:

♦ Pour oil into a large skillet and heat to medium heat.

♦ Add diced raw chicken breast and sauté until about half done 3 – 4

minutes.

♦ Add broth, wine, spices and salt. Simmer five additional minutes.

♦ Add peppers, carrots, coconut cream and coconut to chicken. Simmer 12

– 15 minutes – peppers and carrots should be soft.

♦ Mix cornstarch with cold water until smooth.

♦ Bring dish to boil and slowly pour in cornstarch mix, stirring continually.

♦ When thickened, the dish is ready to serve with steamed rice.

The mightily Habenaro! This small round chili packs a monster punch! Caribbean's pride themselves in their ability to eat this chili. Used in jerk spices, marinades, and seasonings. Not for the timid!

Recipe Notes

_____

_____

_____

_____

_____

_____

_____

_____

_____

_____

_____

_____

_____

_____

_____

_____

Dominican Chicken in Pepper Sauce

4 (6oz.)	chicken breasts	8 oz.	tomato sauce
2	green peppers – ¼" strips	1 tsp.	black pepper
1	red pepper– ¼" strips		ground
1	sweet onion– ¼" strips	2 tsp.	thyme
½ c.	vegetable oil	1 tsp.	pick a pepper
1 tsp.	salt		sauce
½ c.	lime juice		

Method:

♦ Pour oil into large skillet and heat to medium heat.

♦ Sauté breasts until half-done 4 – 5 minutes.

♦ Remove breasts from skillet. Add peppers and onion to skillet and sauté

   until just soft.

♦ With peppers and onion still in skillet add tomato sauce, spices, salt and

   lime. Stir in well.

♦ Bring to boil.

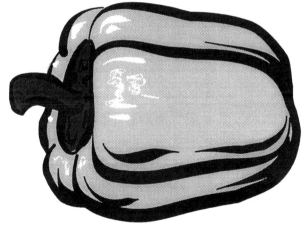

♦ Return breasts to skillet with sauce.

♦ Simmer, uncovered, for ten minutes.

♦ Serve over steamed rice.

Ginger is a tuber or root, unlike most spices which come from seeds, leaves, or bark. A staple of Pacific Rim cusines, ginger's biting flavor is beginning to win over American cooks who use it in ethic dishes and desserts.

Recipe Notes

_____

_____

_____

_____

_____

_____

_____

_____

_____

_____

_____

_____

_____

_____

_____

_____

Calypso Chicken

4 (6oz.)	chicken breasts – raw	¼ c.	butter
¼ c.	lime juice	¼ c.	vegetable oil
½ c.	lemon juice	1	sweet red onion – ¼"
½ c.	brown sugar		strips
½ c.	dark rum	3 tsp.	crushed garlic
½ c.	water	2 c.	pineapple tidbits –
2 tsp.	salt		drained
3 tsp.	ginger		

Method:

♦ Mix lime, lemon, brown sugar, rum, water and salt in a large mixing bowl. This is your marinade.

♦ Rinse chicken breasts and pat dry. Add breasts to the marinade. Marinade breasts one hour. Save marinade.

♦ Place butter and oil in large skillet and heat to medium heat.

♦ Sauté onions and garlic in skillet for two minutes.

♦ Push onions to side of skillet and sauté breasts in same skillet until done 6 – 8 minutes.

♦ Remove breasts, onions and garlic. Place in deep casserole baking dish.

♦ Pour saved marinade into skillet. Add pineapple and ginger. Bring to boil and simmer five minutes, stirring up any crumbs from surface of skillet.

♦ Pour pineapple mixture over breasts and bake fifteen minutes at 350º uncovered.

♦ Serve.

Most cinnamon sold in the United States is actually cassia, not true cinnamon. True cinnamon comes from Ceylon and has a less sweet more citrus taste. True cinnamon is favored in Mexico and England where its used in both cooking and in beverages.

Recipe Notes

Puerto Rican Chicken in Orange Sauce

2 c.	orange juice	¼ c.	cornstarch
2 tsp.	crushed garlic	¼ c.	cold water
½ tsp.	coriander – ground	4 (6oz.)	chicken breasts
½ tsp.	cinnamon – ground	½ c.	vegetable oil
1	orange – rind on – sliced thin		

Method:

♦ Place juice, garlic and spices in a sauce pan and bring to a boil. Whisk mixture to blend spices.

♦ Mix cornstarch with cold water and pour slowly into boiling juice. Sauce will thicken when it returns to a boil. Remove from heat and add orange slices.

♦ In a skillet pour in oil and heat to medium hot.

♦ Sauté breasts on both sides until half-done, about 4 – 5 minutes.

♦ Drain off any excess oil.

♦ With breasts in skillet, pour over orange sauce and simmer for ten minutes or until done.

♦ Serve.

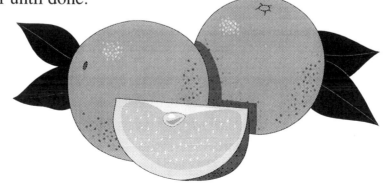

The Caribbean cultivates some of the hottest chilis grown. Scotch bonnet chilis are grown in Jamaica and are added to many local foods. A small rounded chili with a wrinkled appearance. Scotch bonnet is firey hot and must be used with caution!

Recipe Notes

_____

_____

_____

_____

_____

_____

_____

_____

_____

_____

_____

_____

_____

_____

Haitian Marinated Chicken

4 (6oz.)	chicken breast
1 TBSP.	vegetable oil
1 c.	lime juice
1 c.	dark rum
2 tsp.	salt
2 TBSP.	brown sugar
1 tsp.	coriander – ground
1 tsp.	black pepper – ground
1 tsp.	allspice

Method:

♦ Mix oil, lime juice, rum, salt, sugar, and spices in a large mixing bowl.

Whisk with wire whip to blend completely.

♦ Add breast to marinade and place in refrigerator for one hour.

♦ Remove breast from marinade shake off excess juices.

♦ Grill over barbecue coals or under broiler oven until done.

Allspice comes from the Caribbean where it is called pimento by native islanders. Allspice was one of the prized treasures that Columbus brought back from the new world. Allspice seeds grow on tall tropical trees. Allspice has complex flavors which is how it got its name. A primary ingredient in Caribbean jerk dishes, most allspice is exported to eastern Europe where it is used extensively in baking.

Recipe Notes

Callalo Soup

4 (6oz.)	chicken breast ¼ " strips
8 c.	chicken broth
1 tsp.	red pepper sauce
2 tsp.	dried thyme
1	onion diced fine
1-c.	raw shrimp chopped
1-c.	raw spinach chopped fine

Method:

♦ Pour broth into large saucepan bring to boil.

♦ Add pepper sauce, thyme and onion. Simmer five minutes.

♦ Add chicken strips and shrimp. Simmer 12-15 minutes, or until chicken

is done.

♦ Bring soup to boil and add spinach. Simmer 2-3 minutes, until spinach is

limp.

♦ Serve hot

Nutmeg is best when purchased whole and grated as needed. Its aromatic flavor is quickly lost once grated. In England nutmeg in the pantry is suppose to insure a good marriage.

Recipe Notes

_____

_____

_____

_____

_____

_____

_____

_____

_____

_____

_____

_____

_____

_____

Jamaican Chicken and Bananas

4 (6oz.)	chicken breasts
¼ c.	butter
¼ c.	vegetable oil
2	green bananas ½" slices
1 c.	lime juice
½ c.	light rum
½ c.	brown sugar
1 c.	chicken broth
1/3 c.	cornstarch
1/3 c.	cold water

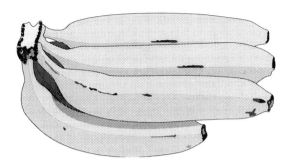

Method:

♦ Place butter and oil in large skillet. Heat to medium.

♦ Sauté breasts on both sides, until golden brown.

♦ Remove breasts from skillet and pour off excess oil.

♦ Add lime juice, rum, and broth to this skillet. Bring to boil, and add brown sugar.

♦ Add banana slices to skillet. Simmer one minute.

♦ Mix cornstarch and cold water until smooth. Pour slowly into boiling banana mixture and stir until mixture starts to thicken.

♦ Return breasts to banana syrup in skillet and simmer for ten minutes or until done.

Nutmeg and mace come from the same source. Nutmeg pods are covered with a nut like shell. This shell is ground into mace while the nutmeg pod is grated for soups and other delicacies.

Recipe Notes

_____

_____

_____

_____

_____

_____

_____

_____

_____

_____

_____

_____

_____

_____

Kingston – Style "Jerk" Chicken

Jerk Marinade

1 TBSP.	allspice – ground	2 TBSP.	salt
1 TBSP.	thyme – dried	2 TBSP.	garlic – granulated
2 tsp.	black pepper – ground	2 TBSP.	sugar
2 tsp.	rubbed sage	1 c.	white vinegar
1 tsp.	nutmeg	1 c.	lime juice
1 c.	onion – diced		

Method:

♦ Add all ingredients to an extra large mixing bowl.

♦ Whisk with wire whip until all ingredients blend.

4 (6oz.)   chicken breast

Method:

♦ Place chicken breasts in marinade. Put chicken breasts and marinade in refrigerator for two hours.

♦ Remove breasts from marinade and shake off excess liquid.

♦ Grill over hot coals of a barbecue – approximately 5 – 6 minutes on each side until done.

Same spices come in twos. Cilantro, a leaf used in Mexican cooking and coriander seeds, used with meats and baking. Come from the same plant. A common spice throughout the world.

Recipe Notes

_____

_____

_____

_____

_____

_____

_____

_____

_____

_____

_____

_____

_____

_____

_____

Cuban Chicken with Black Beans

1 large	onion diced	1 TBSP.	salt
2 TBSP.	crushed garlic	1 TBSP.	black pepper ground
¼ c.	olive oil	2 tsp.	ground coriander
1 lb.	black beans	2 tsp.	cilantro
6 c.	water	2	bay leaves
1 ½ c.	chicken broth	4 (6oz.)	chicken breasts Raw

Method:

♦ Soak black beans overnight in 2 quarts water.

♦ Drain beans from liquid.

♦ In a large saucepan add the olive oil and heat to medium.

♦ Sauté onions and garlic for two minutes.

♦ Add all remaining ingredients except for breasts.

♦ Simmer for 1-½ hours.

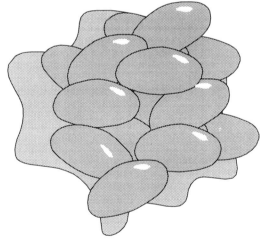

♦ Pour bean mixture into large Dutch oven.

♦ Place raw chicken breasts on top of beans.

♦ Cover and bake for one hour at 350°.

♦ Remove cover and bake an additional 15 minutes.

♦ Serve with rice side dish.

Fenugreek is the spice you taste in chutneys. The taste of fenugreek is slightly bitter with a burnt sugar taste. Used in almost all chutney recipes, fenugreek is the only legume herb. It grows on small bushy vines which produce seed pods similar to peas.

Recipe Notes

_____

_____

_____

_____

_____

_____

_____

_____

_____

_____

_____

_____

_____

_____

_____

_____

Grilled Chicken with Mango Chutney

8 c.	mangos – diced	4 c.	brown sugar
1 ½ lbs.	raisins	1 TBSP.	mustard – ground
3 tsp.	ginger	2 TBSP.	salt
2 tsp.	garlic – crushed	8 c.	malt vinegar
1 TBSP.	Scotch bonnet peppers – chopped	1lg.	onion – diced

Method:

♦ Combine all ingredients in a large sauce pan.
♦ Bring to medium heat – when mixture boils lower heat to simmer. Stir constantly.
♦ Simmer for 1 to 1 ½ hours until chutney thickens and is chestnut brown.
♦ Divide finished chutney into smaller batches and chill.

Chutney will improve in flavor when stored covered in the refrigerator up tp three weeks.

4 (6oz.)   Chicken breasts

Method:

♦ Grill chicken breasts approximately six minutes on each side over hot coals or under oven broiler.
♦ When done, top each breast with one tablespoon chilled chutney – serve.

Chinese

Chinese cuisine often spoken in terms of stir-fry but not all of the recipes listed in this section is stir-fried. I've added a few special ones to the collection so you can experiment a little.

Choo-Choo train rice gets its name due to the fact that this dish is served to diners on most trains in China. Children love it.

If you really want an authentic Chinese meal, remember that soup is always the last course served, not dessert.

Poppy seeds, the blue spice, have been cultivated for thousands of years. Popular in the Mediterranean and Mideast, poppy seeds are used in baking and pastry work.

Recipe Notes

_____
_____
_____
_____
_____
_____
_____
_____
_____
_____
_____
_____
_____
_____
_____
_____

Oyster Sauced Chicken and Broccoli

2 TBSP.	soy sauce	2 TBSP.	vegetable oil
2 TBSP.	dry sherry	2 TBSP.	cornstarch
2 tsp.	sugar	1 TBSP.	water

Method Marinade:

- Combine all ingredients in large mixing bowl.
- Whisk ingredients to mix them completely.

| 4 (6oz.) | chicken breasts |

Method:

- Cut breasts into ¼ " strips
- Marinate in sauce for two hours – remove from marinade.

6	green onions – cut ½" pieces
1 lb.	Broccoli – small buds
2 TBSP.	vegetable oil

Method:

- Heat wok to high heat.
- Add oil
- Immediately add broccoli and onions and stir-fry 3 – 4 minutes.
- Remove from wok.
- Add 2 tablespoons more oil to hot wok.
- Stir-fry chicken strips 3 – 4 minutes or until done.

4 TBSP.	oyster sauce
1 tsp.	sesame oil
1 TBSP.	corn starch
2 TBSP.	water – cold

Method:

- Add oyster sauce to chicken in wok. Next add sesame oil and stir to coat breasts.
- Mix cornstarch and water until smooth.
- Add cornstarch slowly to chicken until thick – you may not need the all cornstarch.
- Return broccoli and onions to wok and mix with chicken.
- Serve with rice.

Daikon radishes have a long history in Pacific Rim cooking. Shredded or thin sliced, the daikon radish has a palate perfect for bringing some excitement to an ordinary vegetable dish. Careful-not too much until you get used to the taste.

Recipe Notes

_____

_____

_____

_____

_____

_____

_____

_____

_____

_____

_____

_____

_____

_____

Mu Shu Chicken

4 (6oz.)	chicken breasts	1 ½ c.	bamboo shoots – cut up
3 TBSP.	soy sauce	1 c.	green onion – ½" cuts
2 tsp.	dry sherry	½ c.	water chestnuts – chopped
1 tsp.	cornstarch	6	eggs
1 tsp.	sesame oil	1 TBSP.	vegetable oil

Method:

♦ Mix soy sauce, sherry and cornstarch.

♦ Moisten chicken strips with marinade and allow to set 15 minutes in refrigerator.

♦ Heat wok to high heat.

♦ Stir-fry chicken strips 3 – 4 minutes until done.

♦ Add bamboo shoots, onions and water chestnuts to wok.

♦ Stir-fry for 2 – 3 minutes to heat through.

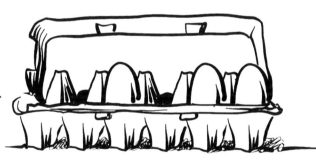

♦ Remove from wok – keep hot.

♦ Heat skillet to medium low heat – add oil.

♦ Beat eggs with sesame oil.

♦ Pour eggs into skillet to form six-inch wide thin pancakes.

♦ When eggs begin to firm up add a portion of chicken – vegetable mix to half of egg pancake.

♦ Fold egg over filling and serve with plum sauce.

Daikon radish seeds-My secret ingredient in everything from soup to salads. A fellow chef from Chicago introduced me to daikon radish seeds six years ago. About the size of a large peppercorn, these seeds impart a mild horseradish bite with earthiness of sprouts or mushrooms. Great lightly sprinkled on a salad-lettuce or fruit. An excellent addition to your cupboard. Use daikon seeds with vegetable soup and somewhat bland cream soups.

Recipe Notes

_____

_____

_____

_____

_____

_____

_____

_____

_____

_____

_____

_____

_____

_____

Stir-Fry Chicken and Mushrooms

4 (6oz.)	chicken breasts – ¼" strips	2 TBSP.	vegetable oil
4 TBSP.	soy sauce	4 lg.	dry shitaki
2 TBSP.	dry sherry		mushrooms
2 TBSP.	water	2 c.	warm water
1 tsp.	ginger – ground	2 TBSP.	cornstarch
3 TBSP.	water – cold		

Method:

♦ Combine soy sauce, sherry, 2 tablespoons water and ginger in a large mixing bowl.

♦ Add chicken strips to marinade and coat each piece.

♦ Place mushrooms in a different bowl and pour 2 cups warm water over mushrooms.

♦ When mushrooms are soft – about one hour – slice into half inch strips. Drain and throw away water.

♦ Heat wok to high heat.

♦ Add oil.

♦ Immediately add chicken strips and stir-fry 3 – 4 minutes, until done.

♦ Add the mushroom strips and stir-fry 2 – 3 minutes.

♦ Mix the cornstarch and cold water.

♦ Slowly pour on the chicken and mushrooms until lightly thick and evenly coats the chicken. You may not need all the cornstarch mix.

♦ Serve with rice.

Don't confuse anise with star anise! Star anisels a strong anise flavored Asian spice popular in Chinese cooking. Normally it is mixed with other spices to create "five spice powder". Very little of this mixture is needed to flavor a dish. Most Americans, unfamiliar with "five spice", initially do not like its taste. True Chinese food lovers crave its complex flavor.

Recipe Notes

_____

_____

_____

_____

_____

_____

_____

_____

_____

_____

_____

_____

_____

_____

Ginger Chicken

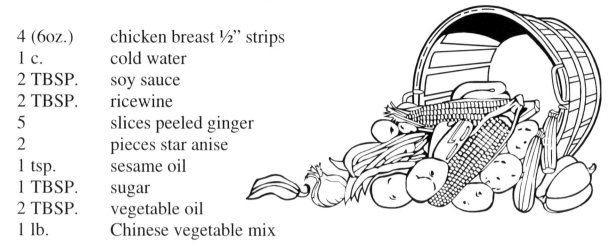

4 (6oz.)	chicken breast ½" strips
1 c.	cold water
2 TBSP.	soy sauce
2 TBSP.	ricewine
5	slices peeled ginger
2	pieces star anise
1 tsp.	sesame oil
1 TBSP.	sugar
2 TBSP.	vegetable oil
1 lb.	Chinese vegetable mix

Method:

♦ Place chicken strips in marinade for fifteen minutes.

♦ Mix water, soy, wine, ginger, anise, sesame oil, and sugar in large bowl.

♦ Remove from marinade.

♦ Heat wok to high heat.

♦ Immediately add chicken and stir-fry 3-4 minutes or until done.

♦ Remove from wok.

♦ Add more oil to hot wok.

♦ Stir fry vegetable 2-3 minutes - slightly soft.

♦ Return chicken to wok and mix with vegetables

♦ Serve with rice.

Lemon grass is important to all Southeast Asian cooks. Until a few years ago lemon grass was available only in Asian specialty stores. Similar to tarragon in appearance, lemon grass gives Southeast Asian cooking a subtle aromatic flavor. Kabobs marinated in lemon grass and other herbs are snack time favorites in the Pacific Rim.

Recipe Notes

Choo Choo Train Rice

2 (6oz.)	chicken breasts - fine diced - cooked
6 oz.	lean ham - fine diced
1 c.	cooked rice - hot
2 TBSP.	dry sherry
½ TBSP.	soy sauce
6	eggs
1 TBSP.	vegetable oil
2 c.	frozen peas - thawed

Method:

◆ Mix chicken, ham, rice, sherry, and soy sauce in a bowl.

◆ Beat the eggs.

◆ Heat skillet to medium.

◆ Add oil and pour in eggs

◆ When eggs begin to firm up add the chicken-ham-rice mixture to skillet.

◆ Continue to cook mixture stirring to blend in all ingredients.

◆ Add peas as mixture is finishing cooking.

◆ Serve as main course or with other side dishes.

Turmeric is a member of the ginger family. Aromatic and somewhat bitter in taste, turmeric gives an added bite to pickles and relishes. Its bright yellow color is used to enhance mustards. Here at Zehnder's Restaurant we use turmeric to enhance and flavor noodles and rice.

Recipe Notes

Drunken Chicken

4 (6oz)	chicken breasts
6 c.	chicken broth
4 slices	fresh ginger ¼" thick
2	green onions cut ½" pieces
1 c.	dry sherry

Method:

♦ Pour broth in large saucepan.

♦ Add ginger and onion to broth. Bring to boil.

♦ Place chicken breasts in broth.

♦ Bring to boil. Turn down and simmer 15 minutes or until done.

♦ Remove breast from broth.

♦ Reserve one-cup broth.

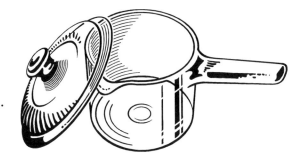

♦ Place breasts in glass or ceramic baking dish.

♦ Pour reserved broth and wine over breasts.

♦ Cover with plastic wrap and refrigerate for 1-2 days.

♦ Slice into ½" strips and serve cold.

Butter is 80% butterfat. The remaining 20% consist of milk solids and water. The milk solids in butter cause it to burn quickly in a hot skillet. If you heat butter at medium temperature you will separate the solids / water from the butterfat. The clear, pale yellow oil is called clarified butter. Clarified butter can be used at a high temperature than regular butter without risk of scorching and burning.

Recipe Notes

_____

_____

_____

_____

_____

_____

_____

_____

_____

_____

_____

_____

_____

_____

Chow Mein Noodle Chicken

3 (6oz.)	chicken breasts ½" strips	1 lb.	fresh cut Chinese vegetables
2 TBSP.	soy sauce	1 TBSP.	cornstarch
2 TBSP.	dry sherry	3 c.	crunchy, chow mein noodles
1 tsp.	ground ginger		
2 TBSP.	peanut oil	½ c.	cold water

Method:

♦ Combine soy, sherry, ginger, and water in large bowl.

♦ Marinate chicken strips in soy-sherry mixture for 15 minutes.

♦ Heat wok to high heat.

♦ Add 2 TBSP. oil and stir-fry chicken 3-4 minutes.

♦ Remove chicken from wok. Set aside.

♦ Add oil to hot wok.

♦ Toss in vegetables and stir-fry 3-4 minutes.

♦ Mix cornstarch and cold water. Pour slowly into vegetables and heat until thickened.

♦ Toss in chicken and mix with vegetables.

♦ Add chow mein noodle at the last minute and toss with chicken-vegetables.

♦ Serve.

Most butter sold in grocery stores is salted. Salting gives butter a longer shelf life and is the taste most Americans prefer. Unsalted or sweet butter is salt free. Used in baking, primarily pastries and icings. Unsalted butter adds a sweet taste to fine bakery products. In many parts of the world-unsalted butter is the preferred choice for the table, too.

Recipe Notes

_____

_____

_____

_____

_____

_____

_____

_____

_____

_____

_____

_____

_____

_____

_____

_____

163

Chicken with Snow peas

3 (6oz.)	chicken breast cut into ½" strips
½ TBSP.	soy sauce
1 TBSP.	dry sherry
3 tsp.	cornstarch
2 c.	fresh snow peas
2 TBSP.	peanut oil

Method:

♦ Mix soy sauce, wine and cornstarch. Whisk out lumps.

♦ Marinate breast strips for 15 minutes.

♦ Heat wok to high heat.

♦ Pour 1 tablespoon of oil in wok.

♦ Immediately add chicken to wok, stir-fry 3 – 4 minutes.

♦ Remove from wok. Set aside.

♦ Add one-tablespoon oil to hot wok.

♦ Place snow peas in wok. Stir-fry 1 –2 minutes.

♦ Add chicken to snow peas.

♦ Serve with rice.

Margarine, unlike butter, is not a dairy product. Made from vegetable oil, it is 80% fat with solids and water added. Margarine has a higher smoke point than butter. The flavor can vary depending on the type of oil used and how it was processed.

Recipe Notes

_____

_____

_____

_____

_____

_____

_____

_____

_____

_____

_____

_____

_____

_____

Sweet and Sour Chicken

Sauce:

1 TBSP.	peanut oil	½ c.	sugar
½ TBSP.	chopped garlic	½ c.	white vinegar
2	green pepper – ½" slices	½ TBSP.	soy sauce
1	carrot – ¼" slices	2 TBSP.	cornstarch
1 /2 c.	chicken broth	3 TBSP.	cold water

Method:

- Heat wok to high heat.

- Add peanut oil

- Stir-fry peppers and carrots until slightly limp, 2 – 3 minutes.

- Pour in broth and bring to boil.

- Add sugar, vinegar and soy sauce. Bring to a boil.

- Mix cornstarch and cold water and add to wok.

- Stir until well blended and slightly thick

4 (6oz.)	chicken breast cut in ½" cubes
3	egg whites
2 tsp.	cornstarch
2 TBSP.	peanut oil

Method:

- Mix egg whites and cornstarch. Whisk with wire whip until well blend.

- Coat chicken pieces with egg mixture.

- Heat wok to high heat.

- Add oil and drop in chicken pieces.

- Stir-fry 3 – 4 minutes and remove from wok.

- Drain chicken and add sweet and sour sauce.

- Serve over rice.

Compound butters – a term familiar to most chefs, but basically unknown to the home cook. Compound butters are butter to which spices and or herbs are added by softening the butter and stirring in the desired spices. Cinnamon / honey butter is probably the most familiar type of compound butter in the home. If you have a herb garden or have access to fresh herbs, you can make several compound butters which can be frozen and used later.

Recipe Notes

Szechwan Chicken

This is a spicy dish.

½ TBSP.	Szechwan peppercorns – crushed
½ TBSP.	shredded fresh ginger
½ TBSP.	soy sauce
½ c.	dry sherry
3	green onions – chopped fine
2 TBSP.	peanut oil
4 (6oz.)	chicken breasts – ½" strips

Method:

♦ Mix all ingredients, except chicken, in a mixing bowl.

♦ Set aside for two hours.

♦ Rinse breasts and pat dry.

♦ Heat wok to high heat.

♦ Pour in oil and add all ingredients into wok.

♦ Toss chicken and oil / sherry mixture for 4 to 5 minutes or until done.

♦ Serve with rice.

Southern Cooking

Southern cooking continues to be popular all across America. Pecans, brown sugar and fruits all play a role in the Southern kitchen.

Modern cooks sauté their foods, in the South they still fry everything. The difference is in the amount of butter or oil used. Frying requires more oil and most often includes preparations with breading or batters.

A few of the recipes call for buttermilk. You can use regular milk if you wish, but the subtle character of the buttermilk does add flavor to the dishes.

I hope you enjoy these recipes, I know my family does.

To make a compund butter, soften butter to room temperature. Stir in the desired chopped spice by hand with a spoon -–do not use a food processor. Place in air tight containers or sealed plastic baggies and store frozen. Almost any herb / spice can be used. Basil butter is great for cooking Italian dishes, while chili and cumin butter is wonderful when cooking Mexican dishes. Whatever spices you use most often in cooking at home are the spices you should use to make your compound butters. Incorporating the spices with butter really helps to carry the spice flavor throughout the dish and keeps that fresh spice / herb taste "alive" in your cooking.

Recipe Notes

Pecan Chicken

2 c.	buttermilk
1 tsp.	salt
4 (6 oz.)	chicken breasts
2 c.	all purpose flour
1 TBSP.	butter
2 TBSP.	vegetable oil
2 TBSP.	butter
1 c.	honey
½ c.	brown sugar
1 c.	pecan halves
1 tsp.	cinnamon

Method:

♦ Mix buttermilk and salt in large bowl.

♦ Soak chicken breasts in buttermilk for one hour.

♦ Remove chicken from buttermilk and allow excess to drip off.

♦ Place chicken in flour to lightly coat.

♦ In large skillet heat oil and butter to medium.

♦ Add chicken to skillet.

♦ Fry chicken breasts 3 – 4 minutes each side – until done. Remove from skillet and drain excess oil.

♦ Place butter in saucepan and heat to bubbly.

♦ Add honey, brown sugar and cinnamon. Stir until mixed well at medium heat. Toss in pecans and stir until coated.

♦ Pour pecan sauce over chicken and serve.

Fresh milk products are identified by their fat content. Milk has 3.25 % butter fat, while skim milk contains less than ½% fat. Cream contains more fat than milk and is sold in four grades: Heavy whipping cream 36 – 40% butter fat, light whipping cream 30 – 36% fat, light cream 18 – 30 % fat, and half and half with 10.5% butter fat.

Recipe Notes

_____

_____

_____

_____

_____

_____

_____

_____

_____

_____

_____

_____

_____

_____

_____

Peachy Chicken

2 c.	canned peach slices
2 c.	canned peach juice
1 c.	water
½ c.	brown sugar
4 (6oz.)	chicken breasts
2 TBSP.	cornstarch
3 TBSP.	cold water

Method:

♦ Open two large cans sliced peaches and drain juice – save the juice. Set aside peach slices.

♦ Place peach juice, water and brown sugar in large skillet. Heat to boiling – stirring occasionally.

♦ Add chicken to boiling peach juice and simmer 10 –12 minutes – until chicken is done.

♦ Remove chicken from skillet. Return peach juice to a boil.

♦ Mix cornstarch and cold water until smooth.

♦ Pour cornstarch and water mixture into boiling peach juice until syrupy thick. You may not need all the cornstarch mix.

♦ Return chicken to thickened juice. Add peach slices.

♦ Bring to boil over medium heat.

♦ Serve chicken with peach slices on top.

Whipped cream can be made with any of the four grades of cream. However, it is the butter fat that gives the whipped cream its stability so, the lighter the cream, the quicker it will get runny. Use heavy whipping cream for best results.

Recipe Notes

Southern Fried Chicken

3 c.	buttermilk
1 tsp.	baking soda
1 tsp.	salt
½ ts[.	black pepper ground
4 (6oz.)	chicken breasts
2 c.	all purpose flour
1 c.	vegetable oil

Method:

♦ Mix buttermilk, soda, salt and pepper in large bowl.

♦ Place chicken breasts in buttermilk mix for one hour.

♦ Remove chicken from liquid and allow excess buttermilk to drain off.

♦ Dip each breast in flour, coating both sides.

♦ Chill in refrigerator for 15 – 20 minutes. Separate floured chicken with

   wax paper.

♦ Heat oil in large cast iron skillet. Oil should be about half inch deep in

   skillet.

♦ When medium hot, fry chicken breast 3 – 4 minutes on each side until

   done. Watch so your pan is not too hot and burns chicken coating.

♦ Drain on paper towels and serve.

Evaporated milk has 60 % of the water removed and contains 7.5% butter fat. Used primarily in baking, its "cooked" taste is undesirble for many uses. Don't tell that to anyone whose just had a piece of pumpkin pie!

Recipe Notes

_____

_____

_____

_____

_____

_____

_____

_____

_____

_____

_____

_____

_____

_____

_____

Chicken Fried Chicken

2 c.	buttermilk
1 tsp.	salt
1 tsp.	black pepper ground
4 (6oz.)	chicken breasts
2 c.	all purpose flour
2 TBSP.	vegetable oil
2 TBSP.	butter
2 TBSP.	all purpose flour

Method:

♦ Mix buttermilk, salt and pepper in a large mixing bowl.

♦ Place chicken breasts between two pieces of waxed paper and pound to ¼" thick.

♦ Soak chicken breasts in buttermilk for 30 minutes.

♦ Remove from buttermilk. Allow buttermilk to drip off (Save Buttermilk).

♦ Place chicken in flour, coating each side lightly.

♦ Sauté in oil 2 – 3 minutes each side at medium heat in large skillet.

♦ In a small saucepan heat oil until bubbly. Add 2 tablespoons flour and cook 3 – 4 minutes, until soft and bubbly. Stir constantly to avoid scorching.

♦ Add reserved buttermilk (about 1 ½ cups) to flour / butter. Stir and heat to medium heat until sauce thickens and begins to boil. Do not let sauce scorch or burn.

♦ Taste - add salt if needed.

♦ Pour about a tablespoon of sauce over each chicken breast.

Condensed milk has had 60% of it's water removed. Slightly higher in butter fat, 8.5%, than evaporated, condensed milk is sweetened with sugar and is acceptable only in baking recipes where sugar is a primary ingredient.

Recipe Notes

Corn Meal Chicken

3   eggs
1 c.   milk
4 (6oz.)   chicken breasts
1 ½ c.   all purpose flour
1 c.   yellow corn meal
2 tsp.   salt
1 tsp.   black pepper ground
3 TBSP.   vegetable oil

Method:

♦ Mix eggs and milk in large mixing bowl.

♦ Mix flour, corn meal, salt and pepper in a separate large bowl.

♦ Dip chicken in egg mixture. Remove and allow to drip off excess egg.

♦ Dip chicken breasts in flour / corn meal mixture, coating each side.

♦ Heat oil in large skillet to medium heat.

♦ Sauté coated chicken 3 – 4 minutes on each side – or until done.

♦ Serve.

Florida – Style

Is there really a Florida Cuisine? Some may argue the point. I do know that citrus and chicken are an excellent match when it comes to cooking.

The slight acid of orange, limes, lemons and grapefruit offers a refreshing light taste that "hits the spot" on warm August days.

Thickeners have an important role in the preparation of food. They coat and carry flavors, aromas, and tastes "marrying" the solids in a dish to the liquids. The four basic thickeners used in the home are flour / water, flour / oil, cornstarch / water, arrowroot / water. All have specific uses and applications.

Recipe Notes

_____

_____

_____

_____

_____

_____

_____

_____

_____

_____

_____

_____

_____

_____

_____

_____

Chicken with Orange Segments

2 c.	orange juice	4 (6oz.)	chicken breasts
1 ½ c.	chicken broth	3 TBSP.	cornstarch
3	green onions – ½" cuts	¾ c.	cold water
2 c.	orange segments		

Method:

♦ In a large skillet pour orange juice and broth.

♦ Bring to a boil and add cut green onions.

♦ Place chicken breasts in skillet and simmer until done – approximately 15 – 18 minutes.

♦ Mix cornstarch and cold water until smooth.

♦ Remove breasts from skillet and set aside.

♦ Slowly pour in cornstarch and water mixture into boiling juice and stir until smooth and thickened.

♦ Return breasts to thickened juice and simmer 2 – 3 minutes, coating each side with juice.

♦ Add orange segments to skillet. Cover and simmer additional 2 – 3 minutes.

♦ Serve.

Flour and water thickener is called "whitewash" by many chefs. Used with meat juices, stews, and some gravies. Flour and water should be used when no additional fats are wanted in a recipe. Extended cooking times also dictate flour and water since high heat and time will break down fats which causes "pudding," fat floating on the surface of a dish. Use cold water and be certain all lumps are whisked smooth before stirring into a recipe.

Recipe Notes

Florida Grapefruit Chicken

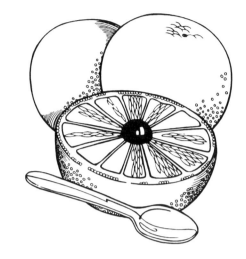

Marinade

4 c.	unsweetened grapefruit juice.
1 c.	brown sugar
2 tsp.	cinnamon – ground
2 tsp.	rosemary

Method:

♦ Add all ingredients to a large mixing bowl.

♦ Whisk with wire whip until blended. Rosemary will float in this mixture

– it will not blend.

Main

4 (6oz.)   chicken breasts

Method:

♦ Place chicken breasts in marinade and chill in refrigerator for one hour.

♦ Remove from liquid and shake off excess liquid and rosemary.

♦ Grill over hot coals or under broiler in oven approximately six minutes

on each side – until done.

Cloves- the spice of kings! Transported on camel caravans, bags of cloves were worth more than gold 700 years ago. Aromatic and spicy, cloves must be used sparingly. Holiday cooking isn't complete without the clove flavors present in pumpkin pie and ham.

Recipe Notes

_____

_____

_____

_____

_____

_____

_____

_____

_____

_____

_____

_____

_____

_____

_____

_____

_____

Florida Lemon Zest Chicken

Lemon Sauce

2 c.	lemon juice
1	grated rind from one lemon
1 c.	sugar
¼ tsp.	cloves ground
½ c.	honey
2 TBSP.	cornstarch
½ c.	cold water

Method:

♦ In a saucepan place juice, grated rind, sugar, cloves and honey.

♦ Heat to boiling, stirring constantly.

♦ Mix cornstarch and cold water until smooth.

♦ Add half amount of the cornstarch and cold water mixture to the boiling juice. Allow sauce to thicken, juice should have a syrup consistency. Add more cornstarch mix if needed.

♦ Set aside.

Main

4 (6oz.)	chicken breasts
¼ c.	butter – melted.

Method:

♦ Place breasts on broiler tray.

♦ Brush lightly with melted butter.

♦ Broil at medium heat 3 – 4 minutes on each side.

♦ Brush breasts with lemon sauce and return to broiler 2 – 3 minutes on each side. High broiler can burn sauce, **be careful** not to have the broiler too hot.

♦ Serve.

Flour and oil is called a roux – rhymes with shoe. Oil or butter is heated to bubbling hot and an equal portion of flour is whisked in. Continue to heat until the flour is cooked and has absorbed the oil. To absorb this roux blends smoothly into liquids. Roux is used when a buttery taste or smooth silky texture is required. Cream sauces and soups, gravies and chowders taste best with roux thickening.

Recipe Notes

_____

_____

_____

_____

_____

_____

_____

_____

_____

_____

_____

_____

_____

_____

Avocado Chicken Sauté

4 (6oz.)	chicken breasts – ½" strips
½ c.	vegetable oil
2 tsp.	salt
1 tsp.	sesame oil
2	soft (but not fully ripe) avocados cut in ½" slices
2	tomatoes – ½" diced
1	sweet onion – ½" strips

Method:

♦ Heat oil to medium heat in large skillet.

♦ Add chicken breasts and sauté – continually flipping breast strips with a spatula.

♦ When ¾ done (4- 5 minutes) add salt and sesame oil.

♦ Add onion strips and sauté additional 2 –3 minutes.

♦ Add tomatoes and avocados slices, toss lightly so as not to break up the avocados.

♦ When tomatoes and avocados are hot the chicken dish is ready to serve.

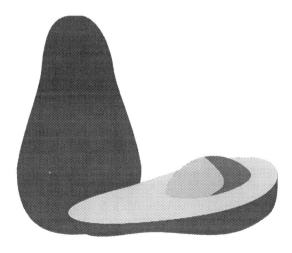

Bee stings and spices-what's the connection? Savory has been used to relieve the sting and swelling associated with insect bites for over 1000 years. It really works! Savory mixes well with other common herbs to form seasonings for roasting meats, poultry, and soups. Especially good with green beans.

Recipe Notes

_____
_____
_____
_____
_____
_____
_____
_____
_____
_____
_____
_____
_____
_____
_____
_____

Orange Basted Chicken

1	6 oz. can frozen concentrated orange juice- thawed
¾ c.	catsup
2 TBSP.	honey
½ tsp.	hot sauce
1 tsp.	salt
2 tsp.	onion juice

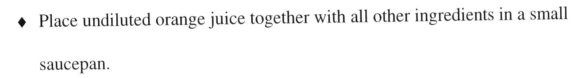

Method:

♦ Place undiluted orange juice together with all other ingredients in a small

saucepan.

♦ Bring to medium heat, whisking ingredients with a wire whip until

smooth. Set aside.

4 (6 oz.)   chicken breast

Method:

♦ Place Breast on broiler tray or on barbecue grill.

♦ Cook 3-4 minutes on each side.

♦ Baste breasts with orange sauce and finish 2-3 additional minutes or until

done.

Tex-Mex

Tex-Mex is a style of cooking associated with barbecue. Unlike the Northern States, Texas Style Barbecues use little or no heavy tomato based sauces. Cumin and cayenne pepper aromas coming off the barbecue grill are clues that you're cooking Tex-Mex.

Prepared mustard comes from ground mustard seeds mixed with vinegar and water. Ancient Romans used mustard almost identically to modern Americans. Several mustard recipes from ancient times are preserved in museums. Mustard also has a medical history. Mustard plasters to relieve aches and pains were common only a generation ago.

Recipe Notes

Barbecued Chicken

1 ½ c.	butter
1 c.	sugar
3 tsp.	paprika
1 TBSP.	yellow mustard
2 tsp.	onion salt
1 tsp.	cayenne pepper
3 tsp.	cumin
3 ½ c.	catsup
¾ c.	white vinegar
2 tsp.	garlic powder

Method:

♦ Melt butter in saucepan.

♦ Add all remaining ingredients and whisk with wire whip until smooth.

♦ Simmer for 30 minutes, stirring occasionally.

♦ Set aside - this recipe will make enough sauce for 3 barbecues. Will last

   3 weeks under refrigeration in a covered dish.

4(6 oz.)	chicken breasts

Method:

♦ Rinse chicken under cool running water. Pat dry.

♦ Place chicken on barbecue grill or on a broiler tray in an oven.

♦ Brush lightly with sauce to start and continue to baste, both sides, during

   cooking 3-4 minutes on each side.

The biggest draw back to flour is that it gives a dish a cloudy appearance. Cornstarch and water is one thickener used when we want to see all the differing foods in a dish and don't want the taste of flour. Cornstarch and water gives food an appetizing "shine". Equal parts of cornstarch and cold water work to glaze food without the thick appearance of flour. Pacific Rim and Asian cooking use cornstarch and water as the primary thickening agent. A disadvantage of cornstarch is that it "thins-out" if held at high heat for any length of time.

Recipe Notes

_____

_____

_____

_____

_____

_____

_____

_____

_____

_____

_____

_____

_____

_____

_____

_____

Jalapenos Chicken

4 (6 oz.)	chicken breasts-1/2" diced raw
2 TBSP.	vegetable oil
½ c.	diced onion
½ c.	diced green peppers
1 TBSP.	sliced jalapenos peppers
2 tsp.	chili powder
2 tsp.	salt
2 tsp.	paprika
3 c.	cooked rice
1 ½ c.	chicken broth

Method:

♦ Heat skillet to medium heat, add oil and then diced chicken.

♦ Sauté 2-3 minutes.

♦ Add onions and peppers to skillet, continue to sauté 2-3 minutes.

♦ Next put spices and cooked rice in skillet with chicken-peppers-onion mix.

♦ Toss so that all ingredients blend well.

♦ Add chicken broth, as needed, to soften mixture. Too much broth will make the dish runny.

♦ Serve.

Arrowroot and water is probably the least used and most misunderstood thickener. Arrowroot and cornstarch can be used interchangeably but they are different. Mixed with equal parts of cold water, arrowroot provides a clear thickening with no taste. Arrowroot doesn't thin-out like cornstarch and doesn't clot when cooked – another cornstarch problem. Arrowroot powder is about three times as expensive as cornstarch, but still costs less than $1.50 a pound. Even in commercial cooking few chefs take advantage of arrowroot's unique properties.

Recipe Notes

_____

_____

_____

_____

_____

_____

_____

_____

_____

_____

_____

_____

_____

_____

_____

El Paso Chicken

2 c.	white vinegar
¾ c.	water
1 c.	brown sugar
2 tsp.	oregano
2 tsp.	onion juice
1 tsp.	chili powder
1 tsp.	tarragon leaves

Method:

♦ Mix all ingredients into a large bowl. Whisk with a wire whip to blend

   well.

♦ Set aside for half-hour.

4 (6 oz.)   chicken breasts

Method:

♦ Rinse chicken under cool running water, pat dry.

♦ Place chicken in a marinade for 20 minutes.

♦ Remove from marinade and shake off excess spices.

♦ Place chicken on broiler tray and broil in oven 3-4 minutes on each side

   at medium heat.

Celery seed doesn't come from celery! Almost all celery seed sold worldwide comes from a small area in India. It's really the seed from a cultivated grass called smallage and gets its name because of taste, not source.

Recipe Notes

_____

_____

_____

_____

_____

_____

_____

_____

_____

_____

_____

_____

_____

_____

_____

_____

San Antonio Chicken

2 TBSP.	paprika
2 TBSP.	salt
1 TBSP.	garlic powder
3 tsp.	oregano
2 tsp.	ground black pepper
2 tsp.	cayenne pepper
1 tsp.	thyme-dried
2 tsp.	cumin
2 tsp.	sugar
2 tsp.	celery salt

Method:

♦ Mix all ingredients in a large plastic zip lock food bag. Close tightly.

♦ Shake bag vigorously so that all spice mixes together and blends well.

4(6 oz.)	chicken breasts

Method:

♦ Rinse breasts under cool running water, pat dry.

♦ Place chicken on hot barbecue grill or on broiler tray in oven.

♦ Sprinkle seasoning on chicken lightly. Grill on each side 3-4 minutes

until done.

Tomatoes – what would we do without them! Curiously tomatoes have only been around since the sixteenth century. They were part of the new world oddities brought back to Europe by explorers. Tomatoes were used almost immediately by the French and Italians. England and America, knowing tomatoes were part of the deadly nightshade family of plants, were reluctant to use them for cooking.

Recipe Notes

Hot Salsa Chicken

1	onion-fine diced
1	green pepper-diced
1	red pepper-diced
2 TBSP.	butter
2 tsp.	chili powder
¼ c.	all purpose flour
2 c.	canned tomatoes with juice
2 tsp.	salt
½ tsp.	cayenne pepper

Method:

♦ Place butter in pre-heated skillet.

♦ Add peppers and onion to skillet and sauté 2 minutes.

♦ Sprinkle chili powder and flour over the top of the sautéed peppers and onions.

♦ Stir and blend in flour at medium heat.

♦ Pour tomatoes and add salt and pepper.

♦ Simmer mixture 10-15 minutes until thickened.

4(6 oz.)	chicken breasts
2 TBSP.	vegetable oil

Method:

♦ Rinse chicken under cool running water, pat dry.

♦ Heat skillet to medium heat and add oil.

♦ Sauté breasts 2-3 minutes on each side-3/4's done

♦ Place sautéed chicken in deep casserole dish, pour sauce over-top.

♦ Bake at 325 for 20 minutes.

Midwest "Heartland"

Midwest or "Heartland" cuisine, as it is sometimes called, is probably the least appreciated of any American regional cuisine.

We have an abundance of ingredients produced locally, which lend themselves to great tasting dishes. Cherries, apples, and cheese immediately come to mind, along with ethnic influences most prevalent in larger cities like Chicago and Milwaukee.

I've taken a sampling of the region to show you just how diverse Midwest cooking can be.

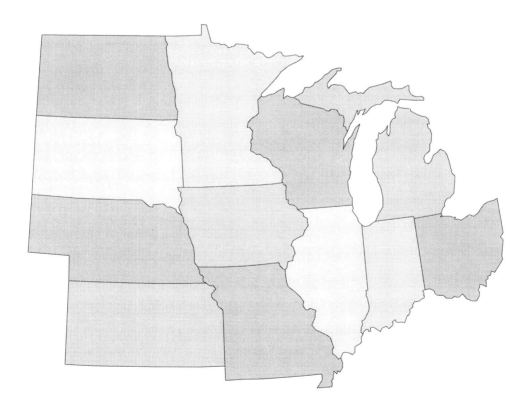

Cinnamon is the bark of the cassia tree. Cut with machetes by hand, only a small amount of bark can be removed from each tree yearly. Cassia trees must be allowed to grow for 25 years before bark can be removed safely. Cinnamon sticks used in ciders and other hot drinks come from the bark on small branches of cassia trees.

Recipe Notes

Chicken and Apples

3	large northern spy apples (3 c.)
2 c.	water
1 c.	sugar
2 tsp.	cinnamon
¼ tsp.	cloves
½ c.	brown sugar
1 TBSP.	lemon juice

Method:

♦ Wash and peel apples, cut into ½" slices.

♦ Heat large skillet to medium heat.

♦ Add water and apples.

♦ Bring to boiling.

♦ Add all remaining ingredients. Return to boil then turn down to simmer

and cook 5 minutes.

4 (6 oz.)	chicken breasts
½ TBSP.	vegetable oil

Method:

♦ Lightly oil baking tray. Place chicken on tray.

♦ Place in 325 oven for 15 minutes. Do not turn breast over.

♦ Remove from oven and place in skillet with apples.

♦ Simmer 12-15 minutes, spooning sauce over chicken as it cooks.

♦ Serve.

Mint is native to the Mediterranean basin. Folklore surrounding mint usually focuses on love and romance. Greeks used to bathe in mint scented water and rub mint under their arms-history's first deodorant. Seafarers believed mint neutralized the sting of a sea serpents who prowled the rough Mediterranean sea. In some parts of Europe mint is still believed to cure hiccups.

_____

_____

_____

_____

_____

_____

_____

_____

_____

_____

_____

_____

_____

_____

Michigan Cherry Sauced Chicken

Sauce:

1 c.	dried cherries
1 ½ c.	water
¾ c.	sugar
½ c.	brown sugar
2 TBSP.	brandy

Method:

♦ Place all above ingredients in saucepan. Stirring constantly, bring to a

   boil.

♦ Turn down to simmer and cook 30 minutes.

Main

4 (6oz.)	chicken breasts
2 TBSP.	vegetable oil

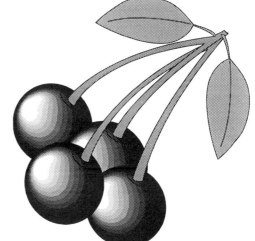

Method:

♦ Heat skillet to medium heat and add oil.

♦ Place chicken breasts in skillet and sauté 3 – 4 minutes on each side or

   until done. Place on plates.

♦ Ladle sauce over top of each chicken breast and serve.

Anise seeds have a strong licorice flavor. In the United States we used anise in specialty baking, while Mediterranean countries use anise for making liquors and other beverages.

Recipe Notes

Easy Wisconsin Chicken

2 cans	10 ¾ oz. cheddar cheese soup
8 oz.	milk
4 (6oz.)	chicken breasts
2 TBSP.	vegetable oil
1 c.	broccoli frozen buds – thawed

Method:

♦ Place soup and milk in a saucepan. Slowly heat while stirring continually to medium heat.

♦ Heat skillet to medium heat add oil and sauté chicken 3 – 4 minutes on each side.

♦ Place chicken breasts and broccoli in deep baking dish.

♦ Pour cheese sauce over chicken – broccoli.

♦ Place in 350° oven for 25 – 30 minutes. The cheese sauce will be bubbly.

♦ Serve.

Dill seeds, used in pickling and baking, have a long history relating to witchcraft. Dill was a vital part of medieval potions. To cast a spell you needed dill seeds. On the flip side, one could ward off spells by making their own potion, primarily consisting of dill seeds.

Recipe Notes

_____

_____

_____

_____

_____

_____

_____

_____

_____

_____

_____

_____

_____

_____

_____

_____

Chicago Style Chicken

4 (6oz.)	chicken breasts
1 TBSP.	vegetable oil
1 TBSP.	butter
2 tsp.	salt
1 tsp.	black pepper ground
1 lg.	Onion – diced
2 tsp.	paprika – hot style
1 c.	chicken broth
1 tsp.	salt
½ c.	all purpose flour
½ c.	cold water
1 c.	sour cream
1 TBSP.	chopped parsley

Method:

♦ Heat skillet to medium. Add oil and butter.

♦ Sauté chicken 3 – 4 minutes on each side.

♦ With chicken still in skillet add onion, paprika, broth and salt.

♦ Cover and simmer for 12 – 15 minutes until chicken is done.

♦ Remove chicken from skillet and bring liquid to a boil.

♦ Mix flour and cold water – beating out all the lumps.

♦ Slowly pour into boiling liquid stirring briskly until liquid is thickened

   and bubbly. You may not need all the flour mix.

♦ Remove from heat and stir in sour cream.

♦ Pour sauce over each chicken breasts and sprinkle with paprika and

   chopped parsley.

Caraway seeds were eaten at the end of Greek banquets. Caraway was thought to aid in digestion and was added to foods considered hard to digest. Today we use caraway seeds in breads, especially rye.

Recipe Notes

_____

_____

_____

_____

_____

_____

_____

_____

_____

_____

_____

_____

_____

_____

_____

Milwaukee Style Chicken

4 (6oz.)	chicken breasts
2 TBSP.	vegetable oil
2 c.	shredded cabbage
¼ tsp.	caraway seeds
1 TBSP.	butter
1 tsp.	salt
1 tsp.	black pepper ground

Method:

♦ Heat skillet to medium hot. Add oil and place chicken breasts in pan.

♦ Sauté breasts 3 – 4 minutes on each side. Remove from skillet – drain any excess liquid from skillet.

♦ Place butter in heated skillet, add cabbage, caraway seeds, salt and pepper.

♦ Sauté until cabbage is limp.

♦ Remove cabbage from skillet.

♦ Return chicken to skillet – spoon cabbage on top of chicken.

♦ Cover skillet and simmer for 20 minutes.

♦ Serve.

Amish Country

My wife and I lived in the heart of Amish area of Ohio. What an experience! The lifestyle of these "plain people" certainly isn't for everyone, but their food is.

Every Amish meal is a feast to behold. Salads, relishes, meats and fresh baked goods are everywhere.

I've concentrated on salads in this section because that's where Amish cooking stands out from any other type of cuisine.

Sour cream, onions and fruits combined in unusual ways give these salads a distinct character. Whether your raising a barn, plowing a field with horses, or just sitting on your patio on a warm summer day you'll enjoy Amish cooking.

Thomas Jefferson and Benjamin Franklin are often given credit for introducing the tomato to the new colonies in America. Both Jefferson and Franklin were frequent visitors to France where they observed and enjoyed tomato based dishes with delight. Jefferson, a gourmet and horticulture hobbiest, began planting and serving tomatoes to friends and guests. Franklin wrote several articles concerning the virtues of "that crimson orb".

Recipe Notes

_____
_____
_____
_____
_____
_____
_____
_____
_____
_____
_____
_____
_____
_____
_____

Hot Chicken Salad

4 (6oz.)	chicken breasts – ½" diced
1 TBSP.	butter
1 TBSP.	vegetable oil
1 c.	celery slices
½ c.	onions ¼" diced
1 tsp.	salt
½ tsp.	black pepper ground
½ c.	sour cream
½ c.	cream cheese

Method:

♦ Add butter and oil to large skillet. Heat to medium hot.

♦ Sauté diced chicken 2 – 3 minutes.

♦ Add celery, onions, salt and pepper.

♦ Sauté an additional 2 –3 minutes – until celery and onions are clear.

♦ Drain off any oil and liquid.

♦ Scoop in sour cream and cream cheese. Stir to coat chicken.

♦ Simmer until mixture is hot.

♦ Serve.

Zahtar is a popular condiment used in the Arab world. Street peddlers throughout the Mideast sell zahtar in brown paper sacks. Here's the recipe: ½ cup walnuts, ½ cups hazelnuts, 1 cup toasted sesame seeds, 3 tablespoons cumin, ¼ cup coriander, ¼ teaspoon thyme, ½ teaspoon black pepper, ½ teaspoon salt. On slow speed, use a food processor to finely crush all ingredients. Use as dip for vegetables or sprinkle on meats, poultry or rice.

Recipe Notes

Lancaster Chicken Salad

4 (6oz.)	chicken breasts – ½" diced
1 ½ c.	water
1 ½ c.	sweet red grapes seedless
¼ c.	walnuts chopped
1 tsp.	lemon juice
1 tsp.	salt
½ tsp.	white pepper
1 – 1 ½ c.	mayonnaise.

Method:

♦ Pour water in large skillet. Bring to a boil at high heat.

♦ Place chicken in water and simmer 3 – 4 minutes – until done.

♦ Drain from skillet, pat chicken dry and refrigerate until cold.

♦ Cut grapes in half and place in large bowl.

♦ Add chicken, walnuts, lemon juice, salt and pepper.

♦ Mix well.

♦ Add a cup of mayonnaise and stir in. If too light to coat grapes and

chicken, add half cup more mayo.

♦ Chill one hour.

♦ Serve as a summer lunch with banana bread.

Although apples are in the market the year around, they are not at their peak from January to June. There is probably no flavor superior to that of the Greenups or Transparents, that fleetingly initiate the harvest.

Recipe Notes

Chicken and Apple Salad

3 (6oz.)	chicken breasts
2 c.	water
2 c.	granny smith apples – diced
½ c.	broken pecan pieces
¼ tsp.	cinnamon
1 tsp.	lemon juice
1 tsp.	salt
1 – 1 ½ c.	mayonnaise

Method:

♦ Bring water to boil in large skillet.

♦ Place chicken in boiling water. Simmer 10 – 12 minutes – or until chicken is done.

♦ Dice chicken into ½" pieces.

♦ In a large mixing bowl place diced chicken and apples. Mix together.

♦ Add pecans, cinnamon, lemon juice and salt. Mix well.

♦ Add one cup of mayonnaise to mix. Mixture should hold together, if not add ½ cup more mayonnaise.

♦ Chill for one hour.

♦ Serve at lunch with rolls or muffins.

Dill weed is the taste most people relate to pickles. The perfect compliment for fish and seafood, dill can also be used to add "zip" to most salads.

Recipe Notes

Chicken in Sour Cream Sauce

3 (6oz.)	chicken breasts
2 c.	water
2 c.	sour cream
¾ c.	white vinegar
½ c.	sugar
2 tsp.	salt
1 tsp.	black pepper ground
2 c.	peeled cucumber ¼" slices
½ c.	sweet onions ¼" slices

Method:

♦ Bring water to boil in large skillet.

♦ Place chicken in skillet of boiling water. Simmer 10 – 12 minutes or until chicken is done.

♦ Cut cooked chicken breasts into ½" strips.

♦ Blend sour cream, vinegar, salt, sugar and pepper in a large mixing bowl.

♦ Add chicken, cucumbers and onions to sour cream sauce.

♦ Chill in refrigerator for one hour.

♦ Cucumbers may make the dish watery if prepared too far ahead of serving.

The ancient Romans thought sage improved thinking and made one smarter. That's where we get the phrase "wise old sage".

Recipe Notes

_____
_____
_____
_____
_____
_____
_____
_____
_____
_____
_____
_____
_____
_____

Poached Chicken and Vegetables

3 c.	water
1	chicken bouillon cubes
1 c.	cut carrots – ¼" circles
¼ c.	celery – ¼" slices
¼ c.	onion - ¼" diced
4 (6oz.)	chicken breasts
2 tsp.	salt
1 tsp.	black pepper ground
1	bay leaf - whole
¼ tsp.	rubbed sage
1 c.	frozen peas – thawed

Method:

♦ Pour water into deep skillet. Bring to a boil.

♦ Add carrots, celery and onions. Return to boil. Turn down and simmer 2 – 3 minutes.

♦ Place chicken and spices and salt to boiling broth. Bring to boil. Turn down and simmer for 10 – 12 minutes or until chicken is done.

♦ Add peas and stir in. Allow to rest for five minutes covered.

♦ Serve in large bowls one chicken breast per bowl.

American "Quick Dish"

Does anyone have enough time anymore? That's why I've included this section of quick dishes. Preparation time is a half hour or less.

Several people have approached me over the past year and suggested that I write an entire book of quick dishes. If I ever get the time I'll write one.

Sage is an unusual spice because you need to rub dried sage leaves to release its aroma and flavor. When you rub sage in your hands it becomes "wooly" to the touch. Sage is an important ingredient in the preparation of pork and poultry. Thanksgiving sage dressing is an American classic.

Recipe Notes

Corn Flake Chicken

4 (6oz.)	chicken breasts
1 ½ c.	all purpose flour
3	eggs
½ c.	milk
1 tsp.	salt
1 tsp.	black pepper ground
3 c.	corn flakes
3 TBSP.	corn oil

Method:

♦ Place chicken breasts between two pieces of waxed paper and pound

about ½" thick.

♦ Dust each piece with flour.

♦ Combine eggs. Milk, salt and pepper. Beat together.

♦ Place corn flakes in plastic storage bag and crush with rolling pin.

♦ Dip floured chicken in egg mixture.

♦ Press chicken in corn flakes crumbs, covering entire piece.

♦ Heat oil in skillet to medium heat - not too hot!

♦ Brown each coated chicken breast on each side for 2 – 3 minutes.

♦ Drain on paper towel and serve.

Always use a pot large enough to hold, without boiling over, water 3 time amount of the noodles to be cooked. For ½ lb. noodles, use no less than 2 qts. water. Bring to a rolling boil. Watch the pot to keep the boil active during cooking period.

Recipe Notes

_____

_____

_____

_____

_____

_____

_____

_____

_____

_____

_____

_____

_____

_____

_____

_____

Chicken and Noodle Bake

3 (6oz.)   chicken breasts – ½" diced
3 TBSP.   vegetable oil
2 cans   10 ¾ oz. cream of mushroom soup
8 oz.   milk
2 c.   medium egg noodles – cooked

Method:

♦ Heat oil in skillet.

♦ Sauté diced chicken 2 – 3 minutes.

♦ Place chicken in casserole dish.

♦ Mix soup and milk. Pour soup mix over chicken.

♦ Sprinkle noodles on top of chicken and soup.

♦ Cover and bake at 375° for 30 minutes.

♦ Serve.

Onions are supposed to be the secret of health. But how can we keep that a secret? To avoid weeping you can pare onions under running water.

Recipe Notes

_____

_____

_____

_____

_____

_____

_____

_____

_____

_____

_____

_____

_____

_____

Crunchy Onion Chicken

4 (6oz.)	chicken breasts
3 TBSP.	vegetable oil
2 cans	10 ¾ oz. cream of mushroom soup
8 oz.	milk
1 can	fried onions (about 1 ½ c.)

Method:

♦ Heat oil to medium heat in skillet.

♦ Brown chicken, both sides, in skillet 2 – 3 minutes on each side.

♦ Place chicken in casserole dish.

♦ Mix soup and milk together – heat in saucepan.

♦ Pour soup over chicken.

♦ Place in oven at 325° for 25 minutes – covered.

♦ Remove cover and sprinkle with crunchy onions.

♦ Bake an additional 10 minutes or when onions are golden brown.

Tarragon called "estragon" by the French, this herb when fresh is one of the luxuries of cooking. The flavor, chemically identical to anise, is pretty well lost in drying. Also in drying, the leaf vein stiffens and doesn't resoften when cooked. So, if the dry leaf is used, it must be carefully strained out before the food is served.

Recipe Notes

Marinated Broiled Chicken

1 c.	dry white wine
½ c.	water
2 tsp.	tarragon leaves
3 tsp.	salt
1 tsp.	black pepper ground
2 TBSP.	vegetable oil
4 (6oz.)	chicken breasts

Method:

♦ Combine all ingredients, except chicken.

♦ Place chicken in bowl and pour marinade over top.

♦ Marinate 15 minutes.

♦ Remove from marinade and place on broiler tray.

♦ Broil at medium heat, 3 – 4 minutes on each side.

♦ Serve.

Tarragon is the "baby spice". Unknown until the middle ages, tarragon is believed to have come from northern Russia. Its long willowing leaves have a distinct licorice flavor. Used in salads and marinades, tarragon is a primary ingredient in classic French béarnaise sauce.

Recipe Notes

Lemon Chicken

2 c.	lemon juice
1 c.	water
1 ½ c.	sugar
2 tsp.	salt
4 (6oz.)	chicken breasts
1 ½ TBSP.	cornstarch
3 TBSP.	cold water

Method:

♦ Put lemon juice, water, sugar and salt in skillet and heat to boiling.

♦ Place chicken breasts in liquid and poach at medium heat for 6 – 8 minutes.

♦ Remove chicken from skillet.

♦ Mix cornstarch and cold water until smooth.

♦ Pour slowly into boiling poaching liquid until syrupy thick – you may not need all the cornstarch mix, so add a little at a time.

♦ Return chicken to boiling thickened sauce.

♦ Simmer 2 – 3 minutes.

♦ Serve with green salad.

Metric Conversions

LENGTH

in	inches	2.5	centimeters	cm
ft	feet	30	centimeters	cm
yd	yards	0.9	meters	m
mi	miles	1.6	kilometers	km

AREA

in^2	square inches	6.5	square centimeters	cm^2
ft^2	square feet	0.09	square meters	m^2
yd^2	square yards	0.8	square meters	m^2
mi^2	square miles	2.6	square kilometers	km^2
	acres	0.4	hectares	ha

MASS (weight)

oz	ounces	28	grams	g
lb	pounds	0.45	kilograms	kg
	short tons (2000 lb)	0.9	metric ton	t

VOLUME

tsp	teaspoons	5	milliliters	mL
Tbsp	tablespoons	15	mliliter	mL
in^3	cubic inches	16	milliliters	mL
fl oz	fluid ounces	30	milliliters	mL
c	cups	0.24	liters	L
pt	pints	0.47	liters	L
qt	quarts	0.9	liters	L
gal	gallons	3.8	liters	L
ft^3	cubic feet	0.03	cubic meters	m^3
yd^3	cubic yards	0.76	cubic meters	m^3

TEMPERATURE (exact)

°F	degrees Fahrenheit	subtract 32, multiply by 5/9	degrees Celsius	°C